Breathe Big
Live Big

A Starter Guide for Your Awesome Life

by Tracye Warfield

Published by bytracye in association with Tiger Stripe Publishing.

Title: Breathe Big Live Big: A Starter Guide for Your Awesome Life / by Tracye Warfield.

Description: New York, NY; bytracye, 2017. | Summary: Self-help book by inspiration expert and wellness industry leader Tracye Warfield with tips, exercises, and takeaways on how to show up big and bold to each moment.

ISBN 978-0-69293887-4

BISAC:

SEL031000 SELF-HELP / Personal Growth / General

SEL004000 SELF-HELP / Affirmations

First printing, September 2017

To Bruce with all of my love.

Contents

Introduction

Sometimes the Universe Is Just Waiting for You to Make the First Move

"You should go then!"

It was 2002, and my closest high school friend and I were having drinks in the living room of my apartment in Oakland, CA. At one point in our conversation, she looked me in the eye and said four words that changed my life: "You should go then!"

We'd been planning a reunion for a minute and had finally made it happen. But, this was more than just a reunion of old friends, it was a wakeup call. At the time, I was miserable. No, I wasn't miserable, I was over it! I hated my 9 ½-year career in corporate banking and had done my best to sabotage it at every turn. And, frankly, I was succeeding at sabotaging it quite well, thank you very much. Can you say, "almost fired"? I was dying a slow mind death, consulting for a title company where my manager also ran a lucrative side pornography business. Ick! I was mourning a pathetic relationship with a man who said he loved me, but not that much apparently, as he had decided to marry someone else. Yeah, not so much.

I had a phenomenal group of super smart, beautiful, and successful friends, whom I loved. But, I still felt like I didn't belong, like I was pretending to be someone I wasn't. I was running marathons, triathlons, and hot yoga-ing my body into a fit, kickass machine, but I still felt like that little pudgy middle child with the hotter sisters. I was over it. I was over being unhappy, unfulfilled, bored, and neurotic—and having that out-of-life breath. So, I decided to chuck my life and move. Not sure where. Just move. My friend agreed. And so, I did.

So, I sold my fabulous Prince-purple Z Gallerie sofa and most of the contents of my super-cool one-bedroom Tudor apartment on the lake. I quit my dead-end consulting job (with the icky porn guy), buried the memory of the guy who married the other girl, and said "see you soon" to my amazing friends.

Fast forward to present day. I'm now on the sweet dream journey of all dream journeys! Today I'm browsing through the latest issues of Bride magazine and hanging out on TheKnot.com dreaming about my impending wedding to the hottest, most amazing king-of-a-man in the Universe plus becoming a "bonus" mom to the loveliest teenager. I'm just getting back from our London-to-Paris summer vacation, while preparing for my next retreat in Barbados. All that after living in New York City, having taught thousands of yogis in the middle of Times Square, and preparing to go to culinary school, just to name a few of the incredible things manifesting in my life. I've grown my company, bytracye, from one yoga class of 20 people into an emerging lifestyle brand. I'm traveling the world, sharing my "Breathe Big. Live Big" practice with thousands through yoga, workshops, food, motivational talks, international retreats, and let's not forget, books. And, most importantly, I wake up each day with a big "Thank You!" to the Universe, excited about what the day will bring. Mine truly is an Awesome Life! And, I want you to have your Awesome Life, too. And, ahem! You can. You just have to start. You just have to "go then."

I wrote this book to help you kick start what I know, and you know in your heart of hearts, is the life that has been waiting for you since you were born. It is my offering of love to you, because, simply put, you deserve it. I know, have met, have taught, and have loved so many people who are walking around moaning about their lives and pining for more, but not actually doing anything about it. Snore! Well, I want you to know that it's time. You get to start living Big today, and I'm so thrilled to be a part of your journey.

Throughout this book, I'll share my "Awesome!" and "what was I thinking?" stories. I'll also share my favorite quotes and mantras to help remind you to keep going. Because you'll need lots of reminders! I know I did and still do. And, we'll get to work on designing your own affirmations, tools, and Big Breath pick-me-ups to spark your journey each day. Remember, the questions and exercises are the same I've used (and still use) to open my mind, body, and spirit to all the Universe has for me, my family, my friends, and all of you. And they work, baby!

This is your life. Hello! Testing one, two, three. Can you hear me? This your life! You are the maker of all the abundance in your life today and all that's coming your way. So, stay as wide open as you can, as you read. Be ready to do the book work, the homework, the breath work, and the belief work to start living (and sharing) the life you deserve.

So, let's get started.

1

*

Dare to Dream? No! Dare to *Do*.

"Life is not to be tried. Life is to be lived."

We've all heard the quote "Life is short." To this I always add, "So, start living!" I made my move 15 years ago because my inner, super obnoxious, and extremely agitated Tracye Twin Gemini voice was screaming for me to deliver on my visions and dreams of brightening the lives of others and living brilliantly in my own light while on this earth. Dreams are great but with no action, they stay just that, dreams. Snore! Everyone who knows me, knows that I'm all about action. I'm a doer. Now, that doesn't always mean I've always been a doer of the best things all of the time, that's for sure. But, I am that person who shows up big, bright, and fearless 99% of the time. One percent of the time I'm the person with *little fear* pinned to my hip, munching on a bag of chips, staggering to the edge, praying I was born with wings to fly.

I am convinced that taking action is like telling the Universe, "I'm ready, baby. Bring it!" And when we take the first step, the Universe answers with "Well, it's about time! Glad you joined the party. Let's dance!"

When I was thinking about making the big move that changed my life all those years ago, I had absolutely no idea where I would move or work. I had no idea what my life would be like once I arrived. I had a sad handful of savings and a whole lot of little fearful reasons to abandon the big bag of foolishness, a.k.a. the move. So, I sat down with a blank piece of paper, closed my eyes, and took some deep breaths (which I hoped wouldn't lead to a panic attack). I said a prayer and then I started to dream and write about places I'd like to live, people who might already be there to support me, my dream job, and even my dream man. Great. I had a dream but still nothing sound or solid.

In the meantime, I kept preparing myself for my move and just began to act "as if." I devoted myself to my then-new yoga practice, which was twice a week, and I saw as a way to calm my mind and strengthen my body. I started going through my closets and donating items I didn't plan to take with me to that undetermined place. I went for runs around the lake to clear my head. I started telling family and friends about my upcoming move to that to-be-named place, and I put my couch up for sale. I was about two weeks into preparing for my move, catching up with one of my best friends in the Washington, D.C. area, and it hit me: I'm headed to the east coast! And so, I was. Thanks, Universe! The dream was coming to life.

When the Universe Shows Up for You, It's Time to Show Out

With the Universe's kiss on the cheek, I stepped up the action on my list with that *little fear* whispering nonsense in my ear the entire time. Oh, that *little fear*! We'll get back to that life-robber in a bit. Regardless, I was on a roll, one little action step at a time. That's how it works.

It's time you start actively dreaming about your life. So, ask yourself: "What are my dreams, goals, passions, and visions for my life?" And then, take a chance and go in. What really floats your boat and makes you want to jump for joy? The answers to these questions equal your Breathe Big. Live Big. Awesome Life, love. Be sure to take note of how that *little fear* starts to censor your answers before you can get them out. Notice how you may start to poo poo or qualify your dreams as they start to speak up. I know I did. And I know I still do. It's part of the journey. But, this is your starting place. To dream out loud or on paper in real time is to allow yourself to see all the Rockstar-ness that's waiting to flow out of you.

Each chapter of this book will end with a Breathe Big Practice and a few Live Big Takeaways. This is where you get to do the work, take action, and step into your journey like you mean it!

Breathe Big Practice

Here's what you'll need:
A pen/pencil and paper or journal.

- ☐ Find a seat in a quiet place.
- ☐ Make yourself easy. ("Easy" is my word to replace "comfortable" which I'm not a fan of. I'll be using "easy" throughout the book.)
- ☐ Close your eyes and begin to watch your breath. Notice the inhale and the exhale as they move through your body. No special breathing required. We'll talk more about your "magic wand breath" later. Just watch and listen to your normal, natural breath as it is.
- ☐ Ask the question. "What do I dream?" It's OK to say it out loud. As a matter of fact, do say it out loud.
- ☐ And then here's the good part: Just sit. Just listen. Just watch.
- ☐ Sit for 5 to 10 minutes (or as long as you can) and then open your eyes.
- ☐ Write down any words, thoughts, images on a piece of paper or in your journal if you keep one.
- ☐ Pick one thing to "do." Yep, we're jumping right in. Pick one! Highlight it, mark it with a crayon, circle it, or whatever works to make it pop.
- ☐ Hold that piece of paper, journal, post-it, in a place where you can get to it and see it daily.
- ☐ For now, release the "how" it's going to happen. Let's just stay focused on the "what" for now.

Live Big Takeaways

- ☐ It's time to take action. It's like telling the Universe "I'm ready, baby! Bring it!"
- ☐ The Universe rewards action with big kisses of abundance.
- ☐ Sit, breathe, get quiet, and dream out loud and in writing.
- ☐ Pick one thing to start the "do" journey.

That's it! You've started. Now comes the fun part where you'll witness *little fear* and all of its cronies—worry, stress, anxiety, and the rest of the gang start to pitch a fit because you're actually, oh I don't know, waking up to your greatness and deciding to do something to turbo-charge your life and the lives of those you touch. That said, I know you might feel like, "What the hell?! I'm not like Tracye or those other people who do things like this. I have a family to feed, bills to pay, social media to play with, and lots of responsibilities. I can't just pick one and do it, or I would have done it already!" Um, yes you can. We're on this journey together. And, believe me, if this recovering Type-A, once broker than no joke, E.W.S. (Empty Wallet Syndrome) having, ex-self sabotager, former not-knowing-her-own-power chick can do it, I'm oh so sure that you can and that you will.

Breathe, love. Just breathe. We've got this.

2

Oh! So, THIS Is
How You Breathe

"Breath is valuable.
Use it wisely."

When I look back, I'm absolutely sure I walked around holding my breath for pretty much most of my 20s and 30s. Frankly, I'm surprised that I didn't turn blue and drop dead or that I wasn't on constant panic-attack alert. Or maybe I was. In any case, I'm damned sure I didn't know how to really breathe and use my breath as the valuable, magical tool that it is. But even with walking around unconsciously playing the I-can-hold-my-breath-longer-than-you game that a five-year-old would play, the Universe still came through for me. I'd get little, and sometimes big, wins in my life here and there whenever I was in my flow. "Flow" means I'd actually take a breath—take a moment to stop feeling guilty, fat, not as good as all my talented, beautiful friends, and so on, and enjoy the moment. However, these periods of being in my flow were short lived. Soon enough, I was back in the game of not breathing.

It was my yoga teacher training in New York where I remembered how to breathe again. My teacher was showing us how to do Alternate Nostril Breathing or Nadi Shodhana, a cooling, calming breath. Yeah, um, not so calming for this girl. We began, and as I started to take in what I now know was a real breath, my heart started to race. It was like my body was saying, "Wait! What the hell is this?" I immediately stopped and decided that apparently Nadi Shodhana was not for me. I was thinking, "Next breathing technique, please, teacher, I broke this one." But we continued with that breath and others, and I kept having the same reaction. "Crap! I can't breathe!" I told myself.

Whatever You Practice, You Do

Obviously, I *did* know how to breathe. I'd just forgotten how. All of those years of my unconscious practice of holding my breath had convinced my mind, body, and spirit that little sips of the good stuff were all that I was allowed. Nuts, right? Isn't it funny how what we practice is what we do? It's not only what we do, but who we become. Breath is everything. Without it, well, we're dead, right? So, in a sense, when we hold our breath unconsciously, we put a choke hold on the thing that makes it all work, and we struggle. Snore!

I decided that I wanted to breathe. I wanted to get an "A+" in breathing. I wanted to be the gold medalist of breathing. That little voice inside my head was screaming, "If you can get your fullest and deepest breath, you can let go, you'll see clearer, and you can actually do this thing!" Sounded like a win-win to me. My inner Recovering Type-A yogini would be pleased. But more importantly, authentic, powerfully divine, and deserving me would be pleased.

The bigger and fuller your breath, the bigger and fuller your life. "When you hold your breath, you hold back the pose" is what I always share with my yoga students. Once you're able to connect with and manage your breath consciously, all of the perceived craziness in your life, the world outside your life, and in fact every single thing around you becomes brighter, and you're able to see through the nonsense and do that thing called "flow." This, I know that I know.

When was the last time you checked in with your breath? Because I promise, if you're reading this book, it may be most likely (and I'm just guessing) that you've stopped really breathing and you're feeling like you're in a chokehold of life. I totally get it. No, seriously, I totally get it. I've been there and I can still go there whenever I forget that I have mad superhero powers and can do anything. And then, my practice kicks in. I get back to the ultimate truth-sayer—the breath.

When it flows freely, it's a good sign that you're on the right track. When it feels stuck, it's time to sit and listen and ask for direction. Perhaps you're going the wrong way. The only way you'll know is to get nice and intimate with your most powerful tool—your breath. Get practice feeling when you're rocking it or you're heading straight for a brick wall.

How do you know when you're holding your breath, you ask? Just take the following quiz:

Am I Breathing? Quiz

1. Did you just take a huge exhale of a sigh at any point in the last few moments? I mean, the kind where you feel your whole-body heave from release. Yep, you were holding your breath.

2. Think back on your day so far. What details do you remember? Not the big stuff, the details. Can't recall? Yep, you were holding your breath.

3. Ever been angry? Yep, holding your breath.

4. And here's my personal latest and greatest: texting, emailing, SnapChatting, etc. Yep. Yep. And yep.

Would you believe me if I told you that if you used your breath (all of it) to move your body, mind, and spirit, you could manifest all you desire, all that serves, and all you deserve a hell of a lot faster? Well, you don't have to believe me. Try it for yourself and see what happens.

Breathe Big Practice

Here's what you'll need:
A pen/pencil and paper or journal.

☐ Take a moment now. Find an easy seat.

☐ Sit up tall and place one hand over your heart and the other over your belly. No, really, try it and stop worrying about who's watching. And if someone is, ask them to join in on this. It's Rockstar breath stuff and they could use a dose, no doubt.

☐ Close your eyes and feel your heartbeat in your chest and in your belly.

☐ Take a few moments in your seat. Let your belly rise and fall. Continue to feel your heartbeat as it resonates through your body. The belly rises on the inhale and falls on the exhale.

☐ Bring to mind your dream goal(s) and focus your breath on that vision. I know. I know! It sounds hocus pokey but try it! Each time you inhale, guide your breath to that vision, to that goal. Each time you exhale, press the invisible mute button on little fear that has, without a doubt, shown up with its cronies.

☐ Sit for as long as you like. Don't be surprised if it's shorter (every second counts) or longer (whoop whoop, you're on a roll!) than you like.

☐ Open your eyes and take a moment to reflect on your experience. It's great to journal it, write it on a notepad, or write positive notes on your bathroom mirror in red lipstick (if you're like me). And yes, it totally freaks out my fiancé Bruce (a.k.a. Bruce Almighty)!

Reconnecting with your breath is a trip. At first, it may seem weird or, like me, that you're that person who's failing breathing class. But it's about starting and practicing, remember? And, being able to tap into the biggest, boldest, super-magical power you have—the breath—is going to support your journey to *your* Awesome Life. Because (and say it with me), "You deserve it!"

Live Big Takeaways

- [ ] Get an "A+" in Breathing.

- [ ] Know that when we Breathe Big, it changes the way we move, feel, and what we do.

- [ ] Sit, breathe, get quiet, and dream out loud and in writing.

- [ ] Practice being aware of your breath every moment. When you find yourself holding your breath, take a hand to heart and a hand to belly. Come back to your superhero life force.

Once you've got your breath flow, you can start laser-like focusing on things that matter, the stuff awesome lives are made of.

3

To Thrive vs To Do

"This is your moment.
Rock it like you mean it!"

A while back, I decided to trash my to-do lists. They weren't working. They were neat and all (actually not that neat), and I had lots of check marks and slashes through tasks. I was so winning at "to dos," I thought. Yes! But, no. I was actually winning at to-doing a bunch of nothing that wasn't bringing me any closer to living and sharing my most Awesome Life. Just a bunch of check marks. A lot of small stuff and lots of "Why am I not delegating this to someone … anyone?" types of to-dos. You know the stuff. Snore!

I was overwhelmed and frustrated. I was headed in the wrong direction. How did I know? Sleepless nights, spiritless classes, dwindling bank account, deteriorating physical health, arguments with Bruce Almighty about everything, and my inability to catch my breath told me so. Can anyone feel me on this? I'm sure I'm not the only one who's ever felt like they were sinking to the depths of a to-do list ocean. This was absolutely not what I had planned when I packed up and decided to change my life all those years ago.

I was up to nothing. A whole hell of a lot of nothing. I needed a new plan. One that did not require a two-page, catch-all list of whatever. And so, hand to heart and hand to belly, with eyes closed, I got back to the breath and asked:

- What do I need to do?

- What do I want to do?

- What will it take to rock this life?

- What will it take to *thrive*? Wait, what? What will it take to *thrive*? Yes, that was it! I didn't just want to do, I wanted to *thrive*.

So why not change my priorities to match my vision?

I decided to create my new and improved To Thrive list. What types of things, experiences, and other such magnificent better-than-stuff goes on the To Thrive list? Think big picture. Think life goals. Think purpose statement. Think life's purpose. You don't have one, you say? You're not sure? Well, if you want to share your most vibrant light and rock this Awesome Life, it's time to put pen to paper or fingers to keyboard and start to speak your heart's truth. This is your To Thrive starting point.

I've shared my latest purpose statement below. I say "latest" because it has and will continue to evolve as I do. It's in flow in the best of ways.

> **I lived a life focused on receiving and sharing love, abundance, and light. A life that inspires and uplifts others to manifest and share their best lives.**

Changing your mind and priorities from what you "have to do" to what you "want to do" and what will serve your purpose will change your whole life. No, seriously! It will make you stop and think about the time and effort you choose to put into things. It will keep you bright, full of breath, charged, and excited to take on whatever it is that will move you closer to fulfilling that purpose.

Nothing is out of your reach. Don't you know how powerful you are?

Take a moment. Go back to that one dream or goal you spoke into the Universe in Chapter 1. Remember that "take-action" goal? Where's your piece of paper, your post-it note, the back-of-your-hand note? If you can't remember or didn't write it down, take another moment. Get still. Hand to belly, hand to heart. Close your eyes and let the breath do what it does best: lead you back to your truth. And you can bet that your truth isn't the 50 things on that to-do list that will never get done, or if they do, they won't really light your fire. What do you want?

Back to your purpose statement. It's time to get something down on paper so that you can see it, feel it, and get super-psyched about it each morning when you write your new To Thrive list. I reread Steven Covey's *Seven Habits of*

Highly Effective People recently, and he sets out a great play-by-play on how to get your own mission or purpose statement down. There's so much out there to guide you on this topic, so I'll leave it to the experts. Head to "The Google" (as my friend Dee's mom calls it) and search *How to write a mission/purpose statement*. Then put some time and effort into it. It may take a bit. This is serious, life-changing stuff, so be willing to invest the time.

Breathe Big Practice

It's time to write your To Thrive list. The To Thrive list should be no more than three to five things per day! Sometimes I cheat and include a few more, but I mostly try to keep it simple. Less is more. Lots of items on the list can create a to-do list nightmare that will suck the life out of you all over again.

Here's what you'll need:
A pen/pencil and paper or journal.

☐ Give yourself a time limit. I give myself 5-10 minutes max! If not, I just go back to that long, ridiculously heavy list that leads to nowhere.

☐ Do a brain dump. Write down everything that comes to mind on a blank sheet of paper. Try not to censor yourself. Just write what comes up.

☐ Next, focus on your purpose statement. Look at the things on your list. What doesn't help? What doesn't support that statement today? What does? Not sure? Close your eyes, get with the breath, and ask the question. Give it a try. See what happens.

☐ Circle your three-to-five To Thrive actions.

☐ Close your eyes. Take a hand to belly and a hand to heart. Allow yourself to visualize those things manifesting.

☐ Let the rest go.

This is not about tossing aside your daily responsibilities of family, friends, work, and the rest. Those are important and should (and will) get done, either by you or by someone else. Hint: Say hello to my little friend "delegate." That said, if you're seriously ready to rock this Awesome Life, it's time to zoom in and focus on what you want, what you'll share with the world, and what you deserve. Are we clear? Then let's do this!

Live Big Takeaways

- [ ] Time to replace your to-do list with a To Thrive list.

- [ ] It's about changing your mind and priorities from what you "have to do to" to what you "want to do" and what will support your Awesome Life journey.

- [ ] Write a purpose statement. What do you really want in this life? How do you want to serve? What floats your boat?

- [ ] Let your purpose statement drive your To Thrive list and your actions each day.

Each day, taking purposeful action that makes you feel good, not depleted and overwhelmed, is going to light you up. You'll start to feel yourself shining brighter and others will see it, too. Now, it's just about staying focused and keeping that To Thrive vision alive.

4

The Vision Board
and Bruce Almighty

"Oh love ... if you could only realize what the Universe holds for you. Go bigger."

It's funny how when you're not paying attention and you start playing the hold-your-breath game again, you can find yourself right back where you started. And for the record, that's not a good thing. That's what happened to me. I'd spent five years redirecting my life to the Awesome Life path. And there I was living in my dreamy, fabulously decorated New York brownstone apartment. But, I was a yoga teacher with a struggling business (to put it lightly), and I was broke as no joke, eating rice and peas to survive, and my head was always spinning with worry, stress, and the rest. I was lonely as all get-out, tip-toeing through the second round of a disastrous relationship, hanging out with friends at cool spots but feeling empty and bored ... the list goes on. This again? Yep. Snore.

And so, it was time for a restart. You see, what I've found is that this whole *start* thing is actually all about *restarting*. It's about showing up for your practice "on and off the mat" every day, gaining strength, and taking big ol' breaths. That way, when you forget who you are (because this fabulously chaotic world has distract-ed you), you have what you need to restart. Time to bring it back to the truth—your truth. You were born powerfully divine and deserving of this amaze-balls of a life. And if you're still breathing and standing with eyes wide open, you can restart.

That's just what I did. Except this time, I added a new tool. Drum roll, please! Ladies and gentlemen, I give you the vision board! Okay, so I know that everyone has heard of and has probably seen a vision board or two. You might even have one already. But for me, this was the first time I really considered making one. Here was the problem (as *little fear* whispered in my ear): I wasn't an artist. Every vision board I had ever seen looked like it was made by someone who had majored in craft-making and vision-board design in college. They were brilliant and beautiful. Ugggh! How was I going to get mine to look like that? Hilarious talk, right? Time to just start … again.

So, I pulled out a piece of flipchart paper from my days as a corporate training director. Grabbed a few magazines I had around the house and just started randomly cutting and pasting. Back then I didn't have a clear purpose statement or vision, so I was breathing and asking the question "What do I want?" over and over again. And my vision board started to take flight. Now, let's be clear, visually it was still a hot mess, but I totally understood where I was going. I had my money section, my look-good section, my yoga section, and my get-a-man section. With a highlight on the get-a-man section. I was again breathing and feeling hopeful.

I put together that first vision board in just a day and proceeded to hang it in my closet. Um, where it couldn't be seen! Learn from my mistake: Put your vision board where you can see it, smell it, feel it, take it all in! Oh, how we try to subconsciously sabotage our dreams, right? Regardless, the Universe once again showed up for me. I started to actually believe again that I could have, do, be all that was on my vision board. I started to make incremental changes in my life to get back on track. I started to believe I could live a more abundant life. I started to get my act together and stop walking around in raggedy yoga pants all day long. Note: I **love** yoga pants and believe they were put on this earth to bring joy. But mine were a thousand years old and just broke down. Anyhoo, I started to network and meet new friends who had similar interests and who were on their game. I started to believe that I deserved the man of my dreams. And guess what? The vision started to become a reality!

Keep Breathing. Stuff Changes.

Enter Bruce Almighty, stage right. Yasssss, baby! Thank you, Universe, for bringing the most incredible human into my life. Wait, no. Thank you, Tracye, for getting your act together, breathing into your truest light, showing up, doing the self-work, and attracting Bruce Almighty into your life. Word! You see, it all starts and ends with your vision, love. Have you heard the quote "You have to believe it to see it"? This is what envisioning a life a bazillion times better than what *little fear* has sold you on is all about. Believe it!

For all the naysayers who are all like "A vision board isn't going to solve all of my drama problems! She has no clue how badly in debt I am, or how horrible my life is, or how I've tried a million times, or how ..." whiney, whine, whine. Sorry, but someone had to say it. This stuff works. It just works. Excuse me, but it just works! If, and this is the kicker, you're ready to restart. I venture to say that since you're reading this book, that you are ready. The vision board helps you to better see and build your "Live Big" plan, because without a plan, you'll be right back where you were. Of this I'm absolutely sure. Take it from someone who's been there and done that.

Check back in with your purpose statement. It will help guide you as you create your vision-board masterpiece. Say your purpose statement out loud a couple of times. Scream it aloud a couple of times, if you need. And then just restart.

Breathe Big Practice

If you've never created a vision board, now's the time to get the scissors and the glue stick! We all know the phrase: "What you focus on becomes your reality." So, no better time than the present to create a picture that tells the Universe exactly what you want. It's not hard, and when you get a group of friends together it's definitely a blast.

Here's the thing: Be super specific on your vision board because the Universe has jokes, for sure! If you, for example, just slap up a picture of any man in the "get-a-man" section of your vision board without specifics, you'll get no specifics, if you know what I mean. On my first vision board, I glued an old journal page where I'd listed all that I wanted in a partner or spouse. And guess what? I received all but two of those things in Bruce Almighty. I can absolutely live with the fact that he really hates to cook and opt for "Restaurant Thursdays." Plus, when I met him he wasn't too keen on getting married again. But I'd called it out, in writing, on the board, so the Universe just took over. Hello! Engaged little mama talking here. Thanks, vision board!

Here's what you need:
- Poster board or journal
- Magazines and/or newspaper
- Photos or images from the Web
- Glue stick
- Tape
- Scissors

Follow these six simple steps to get started:

Step 1: Grab a piece of poster board or a journal (or anything else you can stick stuff on). You might prefer a poster board so that you can display it in an open place, like me. Or you might opt for a journal so you can view it privately. Either works. You decide.

Breathe Big Practice *(cont.)*

Step 2: Gather magazines, website images, and photos for your board. No worries if magazines aren't your thing. There's plenty to print from the internet. Plus, I've also used stamps, wrote quotes, tacked on real dollars and anything else I could find that inspired me. Be creative!

Step 3: Close your eyes and get quiet. Take a hand to belly and a hand to heart. Take a few deep breaths. Okay! I know what you're thinking: "This is vision boarding NOT yoga or meditation!" Stick with me here! Just take a moment to clean the slate. Give your mind a gentle nudge toward letting go of negative, limiting thoughts and letting in Rockstar, Awesome Life beliefs.

Step 4: Take some time to browse. Look through magazines, photos, vision-boardy stuff without an intention and see what jumps out at you. It might be a word or a phrase or a photo. Perhaps you'll come up with a theme for the year like I did ("Turn it up!" was my theme for 2015). Cut, print, tear it out, set it aside and keep going. Hold tight to the glue stick. You're building here.

Step 5: Once you've got a nice collage pile going, it's time to start gluing, taping, stamping, writing, etc. Really, there's no right or wrong way to set up your board. I tend to lean towards sectioning by work, family, travel, and the miscellaneous musings of a Gemini Yogini Foodie mind. But, again, this is your board and your vision.

Step 6: Voila! You're done … or maybe not? Don't be surprised if your board is a work-in-progress, like your purpose statement. Isn't that how life is? It's a journey upon which you continue. So, take your time. Focus on what you've got and know the Universe is delivering it to you already. You just have to open your heart and mind to receive it!

Next, it's about putting your board to work. Top tips on *working* your board:

- Start acting "as if." Show up dressed for your new life. I'm not saying go out and spend a ton of money on new clothes and gadgets (if that's in your vision). I'm saying walk in your biggest light. Put on your best face, and yes, your fancy yoga pants.

- Start talking "as if." A couple of years ago I noticed that a friend of ours would always refer to her then boyfriend as *my husband*. So, I asked Bruce Almighty if I had missed something. "Umm, did they get married while I wasn't looking?" I asked. "Absolutely not," he answered. And then I got it! She was speaking her dream, her vision into the Universe. Love it! Go, girl! And, by the way, they're now married.

- I've already said this, but it bears repeating: hang that vision board where you can see it! I've even heard of people who take a picture on their phone and set it as their wallpaper. Commit that baby to memory. Study it. Mediate on it and with it. Make it your new best friend.

- Ask for help. Talk with your closest peeps and tell them your vision, your dreams. NOTE: Not everyone you know will be wide open to this new you and this "hooey vision board stuff." Choose your peeps wisely. Talk with those who can listen, cheer you on, and offer <u>constructive support</u>. DOUBLE NOTE: They may not be the people you think, as I've found over the years of starting and restarting. Be prepared and open to new input.

Creating your vision board will give you the inspirational jolt you need to restart and get back to the business of manifesting your life's goals. Get to it!

Live Big Takeaways

☐ Rockin' this Awesome Life path is about restarts along the way. Stay in your mind, body, and spirit practice each day with breath and positivity. You're going to need it to get back up and keep going.

☐ Create your own vision board and then work it!

☐ Keep your vision board where you can see it, study it, and fall in love with your future.

☐ Act as if. Talk as if. Live as if.

☐ Ask for help and support from your most trusted peeps.

Here's the great news. You're starting and restarting to take all the action you need to move big energy into your life. Congratulations! Now, you need a real plan. Yep! It's time to get down to business and start to really reap the benefits of this new life you're building.

5

Follow Your Yellow Brick Roadmap to Your Awesome Life

"Set your focus, your intention and build from there. Or, you can wild out, throw darts in the dark, and see what sticks."

I met my sensational, talented, genius friend and marketing coach Gwenna Lucas in one of my yoga classes a few years ago. She was a regular student in my Vinyasa class, and I loved sharing practice with her, but I didn't really know her. That all changed one day after class. She came up to me to let me know that she was moving to Costa Rica to work, live, and most importantly for her, to surf. I loved it! "Good for you and go ahead with your bad self," I thought. She went on to tell me how inspirational my classes, words, and work had been for her and wanted to know if I'd be interested in talking about my business over lunch.

"Ummm … okay"? I wasn't really sure what that would entail, but I was trusting my gut that this was a good thing. Well, it turned out that Gwenna was not only a super-sweet, fabulous yogini and a future Costa Rican surfer goddess, she was a marketing guru with her own company and she wanted to work with me. Yes! This was a very good thing, indeed.

Don't you just love when you're in your flow, energy vibration on 10, and the Universe delivers exactly what or who you need, when you need it, right to your doorstep? Or in my case, to my yoga class. Yes! I'd restarted to make moves to expand my bytracye offering. I was vision-boarded up, yoga'd up, handsome Bruce Almighty'd up, rockin' the To Thrive list, breathing like a champ, feeling great, and ready to take the next leap. I just needed help. Not just help, I needed a stronger, more specific, more focused plan. No, no, let me be honest because we're all family here, right? Well, you see, I never really had a real plan up to that point. Boom! Truth be told, I had no business plan or life plan. I'd been running a business and living life with vision but no real plan to execute that vision. The Universe had been keeping me afloat while I treaded deep water with sharks. And, beautiful peeps, one can only tread for so long in deep water with sharks without drowning or being eaten.

Can I get a "I feel you, I'm totally there/was there!" from anyone? It's one thing to have vision and pretty pictures of that vision. It's another to actually map out what it's going to take to get there. And if you've decided that the less-than-fabulous life you're living with *little fear*, little stress, little worry and the rest isn't working anymore, it's time to get a plan.

New Day. New You. New Magic.

So, Gwenna and I got to work. I wanted something that would lead me down a path that was uniquely mine, that gave me goosebumps from anticipation, spoke to my purpose, and that would help me rock the hell out of this life. I wanted to do it my way with a super nod to what I saw working for others. I knew that my authentic voice, style, and Tracye-ness needed to be shared. And so, we dove into the beginnings of not just my new business plan, or roadmap, as I like to call it, but a map for my life.

At this point, I hope you're starting to see how all this works. First, you hear that quiet whisper of a voice in the back of your mind (or like mine, a loud, slightly aggressive voice) that says, "There's something bigger and better for you." Then you decide to take that first step. Next, instead of spazzing out, you get still, find an easy seat, and relearn how to breathe so that you don't pass out from all this wild new Awesome Life stuff. And then, you create a happy-happy, joy-joy vision board to give you a steely focus on the life you deserve. Next, you prioritize and act on your To Thrive items vs. the silly, nonsense, get-you-nowhere-fast distractions (like downloading that new app). And with all of that, you actually have the perfect makings for your road map.

So, take a deep breath. This is work—I'm not going to lie to you. This is commitment. This will take time. In order to focus, you may have to turn off your phone, put down that fifth cup of coffee, take out your earphones, and even turn off the Wi-Fi on your computer (I know it's nuts, I know, but it's what I have to do!). But isn't your life and future worth it?

There's a great quote by motivational life coach Brendon Burchard that I hung in my office recently. And frankly, every time I look at it, I think, "Damn! He caught me!" It reads:

> "I have to focus now. My dreams will not be realized via distraction. If I care about my family and my future, then it's time to stop being a browser and discipline myself to create."

WORD! This is what it's going to take to manifest all that you glued, pasted, taped, and tacked onto that vision board. Remember that stuff? That awesome life-of-your-dreams stuff?

Are you on board? Ready to make this thing happen? Let's do it together!

Breathe Big Practice

It is time to build your roadmap. Here's what you'll need:
A pen/pencil and paper or journal

☐ Set aside at least one hour to begin. Know that this is just a starting, or restarting, point. And remember, this is your life! Take time to rock it!

☐ Find an easy seat and get still.

☐ Close your eyes and take a hand to heart and a hand to belly. Breathe. Just allow your normal, natural breath to flow for a bit. Feel your heart beating in your belly. Know that you have the power to do anything you want.

☐ Sit for a few moments, focusing your breath and mind on your vision, on your To Thrive list. What do you want in your life? Ask the question and then go back to the breath. Listen and allow the breath to guide you. It works.

☐ When you're ready, open your eyes and get to work.

Breathe Big Practice *(cont.)*

Use the following questions to set the framework for your Roadmap to your Awesome Life.

1. **What's my mission/purpose?** Good news! You've already hooked this one up! That said, you can take some time to revisit and adjust as needed.

2. **What talents, experiences, offerings, etc., do I have right now that will support my journey?** This is where you get to brag about you. You get to call out how fabulous you are TODAY and what you can lend to your new Awesome Life right now. Not sure? Ask your super-supportive, pom poms up, critical-with-love family and/or friends.

3. **What are my family goals? Do I want to get married, stay married, stay single, have kids, etc.?** Get specific. Remember the Universe is listening and taking copious notes.

4. **Where do I see myself in one-to-three years?** Where do I live? Who do I live with? What is my career? Who are my friends? What does my money look like? How am I serving others?

5. **Where do I see myself in 10 years?** Reminder: GO BIG and be as specific as you can. Remember, you'll continue to update this baby as you need. For now, go with your gut. Before you answer this, take another "hand to heart, hand to belly" moment. Get still. Breathe. Ask the question. Listen for the answers. The Universe is constantly whispering, and sometimes screaming, at us. You just have to make yourself available to hear it.

6. **What is my negative drama relationship with money OR positive "money rocks" relationship? And, how, if at all, would I like to change that relationship?** Get real with this and call out any and all issues. I've learned, and am still learning, that our relationship with money has a direct positive or negative effect on how we live this life. And, it's time to stop with all the negative money vibes, right now. It will get you nowhere fast while you are on a journey to build a future that serves not only you but those you love and cherish. So, get your head in the game already! Love you, and you're welcome!

Breathe Big Practice *(cont.)*

7. **Who are my support peeps and how can they help?** If you didn't do this earlier, as I suggested, now is the time to create a contact list. If you have your contact list, it's time to edit it. More importantly, it's time to reality-check yourself on the people you spend the most time around. Think big picture. Who are your future mentors, people who'll get the word out, investors, digital-media masterminds, marketing gurus, etc.? Who are the people that really light up the room in their own special way? Or, who are the people you go to when you need a good hug? (Because you'll need a few good hugs on this journey, for sure.)

8. **What skills or further education do I need right now? And, how do I get them?** If you're planning to jumpstart your Awesome Life, it's time to get schooled. Regardless of whatever countless degrees or titles you may or may not have, it's time to expand your options by expanding your mind.

9. **What are my Rockstar family and friends doing?** See Question 7 for the cream of the crop, and hear me now: You don't need to recreate the wheel all the time. What I mean is, look at the people you know that have a plan and are working it to move their lives forward in the most brilliant and fabulous ways—ways that serve them and their communities. If it's working for them, ride their wave! They are moving in the direction you want to go and more than likely, they are happy to help and cheer you on. You just have to ask. Cozy up to them, shadow them, take copious notes, barter your services for their time and feedback. Pom poms up!

10. **What are three things I can do today to jump start my Awesome Life journey?** This life requires action. No, really. Stop with the sitting, dreaming, wishing-only nonsense. It's time to commit to action. Take a look at your answers to Questions 1–9. Can you dedicate 10 minutes today to draft your purpose statement? Can you call one of the peeps on your support list and ask for help? Can you sign up for the class/workshop/seminar? Time to get to work!

I hope you're starting to see the theme here. One of my favorite quotes says it best:

"No one is coming to save you. This life of yours is 100% your responsibility."

Time to build your Roadmap and work your plan, take action, take detours, get still, ask for directions, fall down, get up, shake it off, and restart as required. You've got this thing, baby!

Live Big Takeaways

☐ Yes, you need a plan! Do the work to set yourself up for your Awesome Life journey.

☐ Create your own Roadmap using your purpose statement and vision board.

☐ Don't recreate the wheel! Ask for help and guidance from those walking their brightest path.

☐ Take action. Get started!

Get ready to feel a big shift! Once you start to map out your dreams, where you want to go, who you want to serve, and who can help you get there, you might begin to feel like everything is rushing toward you. And, if you're not paying attention, that can feel overwhelming.

Here's where it's time again to get your head straight, and the best way I know how to do this is to get still and quiet, let it all flow on through, and listen for guidance and direction. So, if you haven't signed up for the stillness, a.k.a. meditation, party just yet, I'm going to help you out with a little jump start next.

6

Get Still:
My 5-Minute Meditation
Challenge

"Practice not doing.
Life could get interesting."

You may have noticed I've talked a lot of about sitting and "getting still" so that you can get clear. Well, here's a confession: Meditating is, shall we say, challenging for me. My Gemini Type A ego mind screams, "What the heck? I'm a 15-year yogini who teaches people to chill the freak out, for God's sake, and should be an expert meditator by now!" There, I said it. Whew! So, happy to get that off my shoulders.

It took me forever to decide to sit my behind down and practice stillness. But once I did, things began to shift. I began to soften, if just a bit, without losing my passion for the things I wanted to do in this lifetime. I began to feel more focused. And you will, too!

The idea of stillness and finding a physical and mental place to quiet the mind and find clarity is difficult for many of us to grasp when our lives are full. In my case, it is with teaching multiple yoga classes, consulting wellness clients, blogging, workshopping, planning retreats, cleaning house, cooking breakfast, lunch, and dinner for the teenager and guy I love, New York City ... Wait! Okay, so that's my bit of craziness, but you get the drift. It's tough. But, meditation, stillness, or whatever you want to call it is absolutely, positively, and without a doubt a necessary part of your new Awesome Life practice.

Who wouldn't want ease and peace?

"Okay, I get it. Meditation rocks. So, how do I get there, Tracye?" you ask. Well, I'm definitely no expert, but I can share what's working for me and maybe something might resonate with you as you continue to move through exercises in this book at least, and, I hope, long after.

Meditation takes practice. It goes right along with showing up with our Lululemons™ and our fancy customized mat and our even fancier coconut water to turn ourselves inside and out like pretzels in a yoga class. You have to show up and practice. So, set aside (and I mean schedule it, like with an alarm on your phone or something) a time during the day, preferably first thing in the morning when the powers-that-be say that our minds are most open. Find a place that affords you the most quiet and least distractions. For me, it's the steam room at one of my studios. Do whatever it takes!

Here's the challenging part, as maybe you've felt with your own new journey: Letting go. Let go of what you think meditation is supposed to look like and what you're supposed to think. Just begin. Find an easy seat, close your eyes, and begin to breathe. There's no need for any fancy yoga breath. Just breathe. Decide to let whatever comes to mind come. No judgement if you start thinking about how badly you suck at meditating. Just let the thoughts come and go. Breathe in. Breathe out. See what happens.

I sat and watched a guy meditate in Central Park one summer for, well, forever! I thought, "Man! That's how you get it done." Not so for this gal at this point in my practice, it would seem. You might be thinking, I'm good for five minutes max. Okay, then start there. Get yourself a timer or alarm. Sometimes, I grab the $7.99 drugstore kitchen timer I use to bake bread. Hey, whatever works. Sometimes, the ticking actually becomes a form of mantra for me. Take the 5-Minute Meditation Challenge. Just sit for five minutes each day for two weeks. It's a start, and we have to start somewhere. You might actually be surprised. That five minutes might only be one minute one day (Hey, it's totally happened to me), or you could find yourself in a 20-minute sit.

Get quiet. Get still. Get clear. Ask for directions.

The funny thing about meditation is that there's absolutely nothing to do and that's possibly the hardest part for some. Perhaps you're still buying into the whole "work really hard, running around town doing this and that and you'll win" frame of mind? Drop it. Meditation is about releasing the work for a bit. And I don't know about you, but I'm so good with that!

What I realized (and not soon enough, if I'm keeping it honest) was that if I was serious about this new Awesome Life path, I had to sit my behind down and let the answers come. Do nothing for a minute or twenty. Stop trying to figure things out and force the win. I had to put it on the table and let the Universe get all cozy with my purpose.

One of my longtime friends can't be bothered with "yoga, stillness, and all of that sitting." For years, I'd suggest that she give it a try. Then, one day it came to me. She didn't want to sit because then she might actually, oh, I don't know, get clear. She might actually see that all of her big life dreams were still available to her regardless of age, family commitments, and to-do lists. Is this you? Seriously, think on it. Is your ego, *doubt*, *little fear*, and their band of cronies keeping you from taking a seat, dropping your mind's load of bricks, breathing in some fresh superhero air, breathing out what's dark and dismal, and getting filled with Awesome Life juice from the Universe? I'm just saying. Think on it.

And while you're thinking on if you're really ready (ahem, you are!) to start or restart your journey, take the Challenge. If you've been skipping over the previous opportunities to get still in earlier chapters, or if you've been giving them the "yoga hokey silliness" side eye, I dare you to have a seat and let it do what it do.

Breathe Big Practice

☐ You guessed it. Take the 5-Minute Meditation Challenge!

☐ Find an easy seat. Take hand to heart and hand to belly. Or, not! Remember, there are no rules. There is no work here.

☐ Set a timer for five minutes.

☐ Close your eyes and sit.

☐ Whatever happens, just keep coming back to eyes closed and hanging out in your seat.

☐ At the end of five minutes, resist the urge to judge your performance. Just let it go. No one is grading you but you. So, let it go and know that you just started or restarted your stillness practice. It's enough.

Live Big Takeaways

☐ Yes, you can meditate. Just start. Take the Challenge!

☐ Practice getting still so that you can get some clarity and good direction. The answers you seek are in that quiet space.

☐ Meditation is not a competition. Whether you sit for one minute or one hour, it'll be enough for you at the time. With consistent practice, you'll find yourself wanting to sit longer. For real.

☐ No matter how long you sit, it all counts and you'll see the benefits.

7

Move Your Body, Move Your Mind, Move Your Life

"You can get in the game or sit and watch from the bleachers."

Here's the plain truth. The purpose statement, the Roadmap, or whatever plans you've built to live this blazing life you've been created to live will not work all by itself. Fact! Time to get up and get yourself in the best shape of your life for the journey of your life. Time to put down the donut, cronut, and mocha with whipped cream. Time to turn off the reality TV show, get off the couch, log off social media (caught you!), and turn your focus to the fabulous temple of a body you've been gifted. You're going to need a healthy, fit, strong body to take this first-class ride to your Awesome Life.

It's time to focus on the work that will support your journey and give you strength and flexibility of body to make the right moves toward your destiny. There is no Awesome Life when the physical body is a hot mess of unhealthiness. I don't care what you've heard or are working hard to convince your ego-self. It doesn't work that way. Sorry, love, there is no magic pill. You're gonna need to report to duty in whatever outfit (or non-outfit) the workout requires and shape up.

One of my favorite movies of all time is *Fame*, a musical about a group of teenagers at a performing-arts school in New York. (Insert here: my sisters and I singing the soundtrack at the top of our lungs back in the day.) I loved and still love the phenomenal Debbie Allen. In the movie, she plays the super-fierce, sassy, strong dance teacher, Lydia Grant, who takes not one ounce of anyone's crap. At the beginning of the school year, she lets her students know they need to do the dedicated physical work if they intend to live their dreams. It's perfectly stated. In a nutshell, get to work and get the life of your dreams.

Years ago, when I decided to change the direction of my life, I knew that meant not only changing my mind, but looking more closely at what was going on with my body. Wait! We are keeping it real, right? Well then, let me scratch that nicey-nice way of putting it! I was out of shape, past pudgy, physically tired, and very blurry and puffy from too much red wine and pounds of sushi. Truth and snore. Time to get busy.

Although I've always been active enough, I knew I wasn't living in my truest skin. In other words, the real physical me was just waiting for the hot mess me to put down the waffle cone, cell phone, or TV remote and head to yoga class, take a run, or get up and move something intentionally. I needed to get focused on some real physical goals besides "I can still (barely) fit into my jeans, so I'm good!" I needed a goal I absolutely knew would get me charged, keep me motivated, and put me on a new path. For me, it became the practice of yoga. It started from straight-up desperation: I was suffering from a running injury, but the Gemini Type A me was still screaming for me to move my lazy butt. My practice of yoga turned into the "exercise" that started to sculpt and tone my outer body and, more importantly, clear the fogginess inside my head, heart, and soul. Score!

Feeling stronger, happier, and clearer, I was able to envision my life without all of the physical and mental roadblocks the ridiculous ego and its silly little friends try to put in my path. I've got the power to hurdle them, run around them, or (and this is the good stuff) just sit tall, still and peacefully watch them run around in circles all by their damn selves.

Yoga is my thing. I should add, the "thing" for millions of people worldwide. Yes, I think it's all that and a bowl of cherries. And, yes, it changed my whole freakin' life! That said, I didn't write this book to sell you on a yoga practice—although you really should give it a whirl. You might just like it! What I am suggesting is that you have to find your own yoga—the thing that gets you moving, toning, strengthening, glowing, and shedding all the internal and external deadweight and useless negative, cloudy thinking holding you back from unimaginable joy. You deserve it!

You've already started to gain some steam by doing the real root work it takes to get to your Awesome Life rockin' by writing your mission statement, glue gunning your Vision Board, and detailing your Roadmap. Now, it's time to get your workout on, love!

You may be surprised at what that "thing" is. Maybe it's long walks in the park, swimming, biking, cycling, or even yoga. You'll never know until you think on it and try it. If you're sick and tired of being sick and tired (and broke, and lonely, and the rest), you'll get in the game like I did. Move something or not. It's a choice. And I know you're ready to make the choice that sets off the fireworks in your life.

Not sure where to start? What are your friends up to? And if you don't have friends that are in a regular movement practice, time to make some new friends, if you're serious about change and rockin' this life. If you've got movement-minded peeps, ask to join in on the fun. So, what if you've never surfed? As long as you can swim, give it a try! Your friends will be excited you've asked and eager to help. And if they're not, keep it moving. You'll find your workout tribe by just starting.

I remember when I moved back to California from Arizona. I started to hang out with runners. I didn't know they were runners, or I might have run the other way. But they were super-cool, fun, successful, active, beautiful people who I liked. Needless to say, I was the opposite of a runner at the time. But I really liked my new friends. Instead of drinks and dinner, they started to invite me for short runs around the local lake, which turned into longer and longer runs. The next thing I knew, my conversations went from "Where should we go for happy hour?" to "Who wants to go with me to the store to buy new running shoes?"

Check back in with your Roadmap, Question #9: "What are my Rockstar friends and family doing?" Call, write, text, email those who are getting it in. Ask for support. Ask to join. Just ask.

Time to start, or perhaps restart. Once again, I recommend getting still first. Are you getting the theme of things, fabulous one? I've learned that sometimes you've got to sit down (or be sat down by the Universe with a beastly flu, or a heart-wrenching breakup, or a car accident or … you get the picture) before you rise up and act. Get still and get back to the powerful breath so you can tap into what will really engages you and keeps you moving forward. We all know that if you're not into it, it's back to the couch, burger, fries, and your Netflix queue.

Breathe Big Practice

☐ Find an easy seat, close your eyes, and get still.

☐ Take a hand to belly and a hand to heart. Tune into your breath. Just follow it. See where it starts, stops, and begins again.

☐ Ask the question "What do I need right now to get moving?" Seriously! Ask the question. And then sit with it. See what images come up. Listen to the first thought that flows in. Whether it's "Train to run a marathon" or "Start by walking to the mailbox each morning." Whatever it is, go with it. Start with it. Restart with it.

What I've learned is that there really isn't a wrong action. It's all just gently, or not so gently, placed under the category of learning — learning what works for you and what serves you and your body.

Live Big Takeaways

☐ Get moving! You're going to need to be in the best shape possible to rock this Awesome Life!"

☐ Find your "Get fit and fabulous thing." Get still and ask the question and see what speaks to you. Then, take action.

☐ Keep it real. Know that this is a whole body, mind, spirit thing. When one is out of whack, bloated, and exhausted, the rest of you suffers.

☐ Remind yourself you are a superhero Rockstar and you deserve to feel amazing — mind, body, and soul.

Warning! As you start to move and change, you're no longer going to crave, want, or need those things, places, and people (yes, I said it) that don't serve your bigger purpose to brighten your path and serve others. And that, my love, could get quite uncomfortable. Good! That said, I'm not a fan of pain, and neither should you be, so know that "uncomfortable" means you're growing, learning, and setting yourself up to live and give of your most abundant, spectacular self.

8

Time to Drop the Dead Weight or Sink With It

"Once you spread your wings, nothing can hold you down but you."

It was June 2010 when I slammed head first into another monster brick wall on my journey. I was on round two of a hot mess of a relationship with someone I had no business fooling with. Round one of the relationship ended with a midday call on my business phone from a calm, lovely lady who claimed she was his long-time partner and mother to his adorable young daughter and who wanted to "understand" our relationship. Well, for most sane, self-loving, bright people, that would have been it, right? Not for me. I had let him back into my life. In other words, I had once again slipped back into Awesome Life sabotage and hold-my-breath-like-a-five-year-old mode.

I was ripe for a knight-in-shining-armor to come and save me from my miserable existence. Isn't it interesting when you're all about being saved from a situation, the Universe says, "OK, so you think this is a knight-in-shining-armor deal? Okey dokie. Well, that's not how it works. I'll just give you this and maybe because 'this' is a hot mess, you'll realize YOU are your own knight-in-shining-armor. I love you. Go with it and let me know how that works for ya." Imagine a chuckle from the Universe and a big ol' snore.

Enter monster brick wall. I hit it hard when I had to realize this mess was just that—a mess, and I had to let it go. Albeit, it was a bit easier with round two, interestingly enough. I was back on breath and it all made sense. Let it go. Not working. Let it go. You deserve better. Goodbye, non-relationship deadweight.

In addition to the relationship, I was in my fourth year of a corporate job, where I was managing things and people, traveling, and living in hotel suites. I was, by all accounts, successful but miserable. No, really, I was in complete misery, as well as bored, lonely, and completely unfulfilled. I mean, I showed up and rocked it every day. I was a Rockstar at my job. And I hated it. All of it. No, really, all of it.

That relationship exit was a catalyst. About a month after dissolving the "mess", I decided, as I sat alone in a New Jersey hotel suite that I was done with my "fantastic" corporate job where I traveled, met interesting people, and made a bucket-load of money. Time to quit the job I absolutely did not love so I could do something that would give me joy. And so, I did. Goodbye, job-that no-longer-floats-my-boat deadweight.

I was starting to shake off things that felt heavy and were holding me back from my light. I honestly could feel myself getting lighter with each shake.

I'm reminded of my marathon running days. I could never carry all those gadgets, backpacks, water bottles, sports drinks, goo, etc. They were just too heavy. The race was way too long and hard for all that crap. I felt weighed down at a time when I needed to feel like I could fly.

Drop it! In my first long race years ago, I remember tossing stuff along the roadside. I had to get lighter and keep moving to the finish line. Relying on my mental strength, my team, and the volunteers at the water stops was my only choice.

In yoga class, people arrive and set up their spot with a fancy mat, 18 water bottles, a special towel, and anything else they can find to get the perfect flow. Perhaps distractions? A little deadweight? I'm just saying. Drop it!

As you look at your life, ask yourself, "How much deadweight am I carrying?" What's got to go?

On a recent trip a beloved friend reminded me to question the value of people, events, and possessions in my life. Is there someone, something, some place holding you back from your true self? Your destiny? Your peace? Your freedom?

So, how do you know when you're being emotionally or physically dragged down by deadweight and sinking?

- **You feel stalled or "stuck" (keep in mind that I wish I could remove stuck from the dictionary).** There doesn't seem to be any forward motion in your life, and you're starting to feel like everything is déjà vu ("Haven't I been here/seen this before?"), but not in a good way.

- **Your close family and friends tell you.** In my case, it's my BFF Betsy. She's good for a "What the hell!" call to say, "You're drowning, girl, enough already!"

- **Your close family and friends stop telling you.** Sinking alert! When the calls, emails, texts, and get-togethers become few and far in between, you've got a problem. You've become isolated from your peeps or they've isolated themselves from you because you've become a hot fiery mess of pitiful and they can't save you from the darkness you created and aren't interested in being pulled down the rabbit hole with you.

To cut the anchor means two things. First, you have to know it's too heavy and you weren't born to sink to the bottom. Second:

You've got to fluff up your Rockstar wings baby. It's time to fly!

You have to start or restart somewhere by setting yourself free of what does not lift you and, therefore, does not help you live in your purpose.

Here are a few suggestions from someone who stays in the active "Drop it!" state:

- **Get with your Real Team.** Who are the people who keep it real in your life? Who will honestly and out of true love tell you when you're wrong, someone is wrong for you, or something is wrong. Go back to your Roadmap "Who are my Rockstar Peeps?" question. Ask, listen, and do.

- **Be honest with yourself.** It's hard and exhausting to toss all deadweight at once. Trust me on this one. Take it a pound at a time. One thought, one action, one decision to free yourself, at a time.

- **Stay on the lookout for volunteers and water stops along the way.** If we pay attention, we will find help and cheers available everywhere. There are so many people who want you to soar, some you may not even know yet or ever. You need them.

- **Go to the Divine.** Humble yourself and know there is a greater source. Allow yourself to be guided.

Breathe Big Practice

Here's what you'll need:
A pen/pencil, a notebook, piece of paper, or journal
You can also use a timer or alarm if you'd like. Start with one minute or go as long as you want. It all counts!

- ☐ Find a quiet place to sit. This really does require a quiet spot, even if it means finding a corner or a closet in your house or apartment. Or, it could be your local library among the stacks or outside in a park, but go someplace distraction-free by yourself.

- ☐ Keep your pen/pencil and paper close by. You'll use them shortly.

- ☐ Close your eyes and take a hand to belly and a hand to heart. Breathe. Just allow whatever breath comes and goes to happen without grading or judging. Follow the breath and just notice, perhaps, where it falters, stops, or feels light or heavy. Just watch it for a bit.

- ☐ Keeping your eyes closed, begin to focus on your exhale.

- ☐ With each exhale, allow yourself to say, "Let go" in your mind. Inhale, exhale. "Let go." Continue until your alarm rings.

- ☐ Keep your eyes closed and release your arms to your side. Just take a moment and let your mind do whatever it wants and notice any pictures, feelings, or thoughts that run through your head.

- ☐ Open your eyes and take a moment to write down how you feel, any thoughts, words, phrases, pictures, or scenes that came to mind. You'll be surprised at how once you actually start to say, "Let go" and speak it to yourself and into the Universe, how apparent what's not working and what's not serving will become, either immediately or with consistent practice and time.

You don't have to know how you will let go. You just have to be willing to practice sitting still with it and realizing, through the stillness, that it bites, it's no longer for you, or never was in the first place. The answers and solutions come with practice. Take it from me, as I fluff my Rockstar wings, that this stuff works.

Breathe Big Practice *(cont.)*

I want you to discover and know, as I have, you are not alone and are not required to carry the deadweight of the world on your shoulders. That's not your job or anybody's, for that matter. Your job is to soar. Your job is to live a life full of love, abundance, and light. That does not include moldy, old, heartbreaking, back-breaking anchors that take the whole ship down. Not for you. Period. End of story. That's all, folks.

Live Big Takeaways

- ☐ Decide to get clear on the things, situations, and, yes, people, which make you feel heavy or stuck.

- ☐ Revisit your purpose statement, Roadmap, and Vision Board for "eyes on the prize" focus and to stay inspired.

- ☐ Practice the Let Go breath regularly. Take note of what comes up and begin to take "Drop it" action.

Take it from me. It feels amazing to walk lighter once you've released whatever it is that holds you back. Only you know what that "it" is. Take a long look. Practice seeing it, calling it out by its name, and leaving it behind. It's not for you.

9

The Moment You Know That You Know and Then You Don't

"Give doubt a hug.
Then take a deep breath and keep going."

D*oubt* is the second cousin twice removed from *little fear*. And, like *little fear*, *doubt* loves to hang in your left ear with little whispers of "Hmmm, not sure you can do that, baby. You'll need lots more money, time, blah, blah, blah," especially when you are excited about your purpose statement, Roadmap, and brand-new plan to get body and head in the game. Then, in the quiet moments of the night or early morning, *doubt's* happy hours, it starts to sing its songs of "You failed in the past when you tried this or that," or "Everyone will laugh at you," and "This stuff is for other people who are real Rockstars, not a fraud like you."

My first book was a 49-page cookbook called *Experience Dinner: Recipes by Tracye Warfield*. Not quite *The Joy of Cooking*, that's for sure. Anyway, I'm no chef, but my Auntie Sandra thought I was a really good cook and told me I should write a cookbook, so there you go. I thought, "That's a great idea!" And my Gemini Type A Yogini on the path mind said, "Yes! Add one more thing to your already stuffed plate of randomness and write that damn cookbook, girl!" I was jazzed. But that 49-page cookbook didn't happen for another three years. Somewhere between a glass of wine with my aunt and my plans, *doubt* took hold. Who was I to write a cookbook? No one would buy it or read it, for sure. This was something that professional chefs, the real Rockstars did, not me. So, I put it on the back burner and continued with the safe stuff on my plate, checking off my never-ending, non-threatening, going-nowhere-fast To-Do list of bull.

You see that's what *doubt* does. If you listen and let it, it will happily lead you right back to that place of non-awesomeness, otherwise known as mediocrity. It's that place right before your big Awesome Life breakthrough. You get to go directly back to piddling around your ho-hum life, broke as no joke, trolling dating sites, procrastinating, and giggling at GIFs of babies eating spaghetti, while *doubt* grins and whispers, "You're welcome." Snore.

That's exactly what happened to me for three years until I pushed the "restart" button again, one cold, snowy Sunday. After yoga class, I decided to get up and start my book. It wasn't that *doubt* had disappeared. I decided to "practice" writing a book. Just like my class, I was going to take it one pose, one breath, one discomfort, one "oh hell yeah, that feels good" at a time. I didn't really know how; I just took a deep breath and began. And then I just kept going.

I've become good friends with *doubt*. Its cousin *little fear*, not so much, but we're working on our relationship. But, *doubt* and I have an understanding. It can hang out, whisper, and sing all it likes. I will nod politely and proceed with moving forward and taking action. It's welcome to take the ride and shut the hell up or go find another bar for its happy hour antics. Smooches and Namaste. You see, it's silly to pick a fight with *doubt*. It's futile. Instead, you can decide to see it, acknowledge it, freak out for a moment if you must, and then get up and keep moving.

A few tips on how to move with *doubt*:

First, tap back into your inspiration—your purpose statement, your Vision Board, and your Roadmap. Remember your goals and Rockstar dreams and why they're important to you. That's why you've got to have these things visible. Hang 'em where you can see 'em. Set your ringtone with your voice reciting your purpose. Take a picture of your Vision Board and make it your screensaver. Set up a coffee talk, FaceTime, or Skype with one of your Rockstar Peeps and chat about your Roadmap. Get giddy enough to want to jump out of your seat with joy about this Awesome Life path you're on. Let the pom poms up cheer become the only real voice you hear in those wee hours.

Decide that action is practice. Your job is to practice one little (or big) thing at a time. And here's the real kicker! You get to practice with *doubt*. In fact, you get to train not only yourself, but your new BFF *doubt*, on how you will take action, not in spite of it, but arm-in-arm with it. Practice saying "yes" to one thing at a time and decide to focus on just being in that moment.

Just keep moving forward.

Move your body! There's nothing like exercise, in whatever form you've decided to knock the venom out of *doubt* (because I know that you've decided to get off the couch and get in the game, right?). The stronger, brighter, and more energized you become in body, the more you can recharge your mind and spirit to bear-hug *doubt*, sit it down in its little corner, and give it a video game to play while we get on with the big bold, world-is-your-oyster type of living.

Keep breathing, huge-like. All the naysaying voices in our head rise up when we constrict the gift that keeps our lungs pumping, our heart beating, and opportunities flowing to rock our lives and the lives of others. The naysaying voices love it when we get in our doubtful, the-Universe-is-definitely-not-supporting-me heads to hold our breath and wait to pass out so we don't have to deal or try or win or grow. This is when we need to whisper (or holler), "Let go" with every exhale and "You've got this!" with every inhale. (And yes, I practice this regularly, sometimes successfully and sometimes not.) When we do this, the naysaying voices find their way to the back seat. So, keep breathing, huge-like.

Breathe Big Practice

Here's what you'll need:
A place to walk around, i.e., a park, the block, around your house, etc.

☐ Here's a change! This time we breathe and walk. Some call it walking meditation. You can call it whatever you like. But, it's time to sync your breath with action and practice walking with *doubt*.

☐ I love a 20-minute walk. It's just enough for me to get out of my head, into my light, and wake up my body. I'm fortunate enough to live by one of the most beautiful parks in the world, Central Park in New York, but you can choose any place. If a treadmill is your park of the day, then so be it. If you have to walk in circles around your house or apartment, well that works, too. The goal is to find a place to move your breath and your body.

☐ To begin, while standing, take a hand to belly and a hand to heart this time with your eyes open. Just breathe for a bit, taking it all in, wherever you are. Just let the sights and sounds wash over you. No, really, even in your living room if that's where you landed. And if you are in a public place, a big "who cares" to who's watching! This is your Awesome Life we're talking about. Are you in the game or back on the couch sidelines? Plus, and believe me, you're serving others by example.

☐ Take a deep breath in, and as you do, say to yourself, "You've got this!" and as you exhale, "Let go." Do this a few times and then begin. I try not to walk with music so that I really stay present and practice my "Let go" and "You've got this" breaths. But, if music floats your boat and gets you rockin', by all means let it flow.

☐ Post-walk, take a moment to sit. Close your eyes and just take a moment to listen and feel the sensations in your mind and body. Let the work, the action sink in. Let go. You've got this.

Live Big Takeaways

- [ ] Dull *doubt's* happy hour song and dance by staying in tune, in touch, and inspired by your purpose, your vision, your plan.

- [ ] Decide to walk, run, and/or skip towards your goals with *doubt* riding in the back seat. Know that your will and practice will keep you moving forward.

- [ ] Remember that your breakthrough, your Awesome Life party, is waiting for you. Your job is to stay in action.

Know that resisting *doubt* won't get you far. You'll just end up feeling stuck. The key is to roll with it, to let go of the fight, to let it wash over you or to even ride with you on your journey. Your job? Keep going!

10

Heed the Potato Chip Lady's Advice

"The struggle is NOT real. Let it go."

A while back I took the 1 subway train to the South Ferry station to teach one of my yoga classes. I never take the 1 train to that location. Anyhoot, I took the 1 train because, this time, a little, sweet voice in my head told me to, you know: "Take the 1 train." For once, I was thankful not to be hollered at by my inner voice.

I'm riding along in a packed subway car. We stop at a station and a woman steps in and squeezes her way to the only seat left, next to me. She's holding a bag with her whole lunch, preparing to whip it out and eat the entire meal on the train. "Ugggggh!" I quietly groaned (or my big ol' ego groaned). But to my ego's amazement, she simply pulled out a small bag of chips, unfolded a piece of crumpled paper, and began to read while munching. I couldn't help but glance over to see what she was reading, and what a gift I got!

As the train reached my station, I asked politely if I could snap a picture of the paper she was reading. She looked at me, smiled, and said, "Oh no bother, as soon as I finish reading this last sentence, THIS is for you!" Again, what a gift!

There's no better time than the present to share "Some Words of Wisdom to Live By": The List, from the Potato Chip Lady, because, apparently, I was supposed to take a train I never take, sit by that lovely lady, and receive this message to share. So here goes:

- Life isn't fair, but it is still good.
- Time heals almost everything, so give time, time.
- Don't compare your life to others. You have no idea what their journey is all about.
- You don't have to win every argument. Agree to disagreements.
- Get rid of anything that isn't useful, beautiful, or joyful.
- Try to make at least three people smile each day.
- Each night before you go to bed, complete these statements: 1) I am thankful for … and 2) Today I accomplished …
- Call your family often.
- Take a 10-to-30-minute walk every day, and while you walk, smile.
- Forgive everyone for everything.
- Dream more while you are awake.
- What other people think of you is none of your business.
- Sit in silence for at least 10 minutes every day.
- Enjoy the ride. Remember this is not Disney World and you certainly don't want a fast pass. Make the most of it, and enjoy the ride.
- Smile and laugh more. It will keep the energy vampires away.
- Don't take yourself so seriously; no one else does.
- Realize that life is a school and you are here to learn. Pass all your tests. Problems are simply part of the curriculum that appear and fade away like algebra class, but the lessons you learn will last a lifetime.
- Your job won't take care of you when you are sick. Your friends will. Stay in touch.
- No one is in charge of your happiness but you.
- Life is too short to waste time hating anyone.
- Spend more time with people over the age of 70 and under the age of 6.
- When you wake up in the morning, complete the statement: My purpose is _____ today.
- Remember that you are too blessed to be stressed.
- No matter how you feel, get up, dress up, and show up.
- The best is yet to come. BELIEVE!
- Burn the candles, use the nice sheets. Don't save them for a special occasion. Today is special.
- Make peace with your past, so it won't mess up your present. However good or bad a situation is, it will change.

- Live with the three Es: Energy, Enthusiasm, and Empathy; and the three Fs: Faith, Family, and Friends.

And, boom! Pretty much sums it all up, right? Honestly, this list IS your Roadmap.

I spent the next week sharing this with every single person I ran into, taught, consulted, hugged, kissed, and all that jazz. I place it at the top of "a few of my favorite things" list, because although I'd heard many of these sayings before, it was a good reminder that this Awesome Life stuff is pretty simple.

And it is. Simple. Just getting back to basics. Life Lessons 101. Do this, and it's all good. Don't you just love how the Universe drops these little nuggets in our lives when we start showing up to play like we mean it, do the work, focus on what and who matter the most and begin to blossom in our truest light? It's like a stamp of approval and big ol' pom poms up at the same time.

This list is struggle-free. It's singing the "Let go. You've got this" theme song all the way through. And, if nothing in this book has hit home for you, let me offer you the most important lesson I've learned to date in my life's journey:

You have to let go to let in.

You're doing all the breathing, sitting, moving, planning, and envisioning the Awesome Life that you absolutely, 100 percent, without a doubt, deserve. But, are you willing to actively shed the silly, and not so silly, stuff that's taking up space and making this ride a lot bumpier and more uncomfortable than it's supposed to be, even downright painful? I'm betting that you are.

But, I get it. I totally get it. Been there and done all of the silly, uncomfortable, and painful stuff a zillion times. And, it bites. Especially, when it's ridiculously simple. No, seriously. I'm finding that out more and more every day, and I hope that you are too as we take this journey together.

"THIS is for you," said the Potato Chip Lady. Ahem! Time to start or restart, and with a smile on your face and an open heart. The life you deserve is waiting. Let's enjoy the ride together.

Breathe Big Practice

Here's what you'll need:
A pen/pencil and paper or journal.

☐ Take the Potato Chip Lady's advice and get still for 10 minutes. You may want to have a piece of paper and pen to jot down some thoughts after.

☐ Find an easy seat. Close your eyes. Take hand to belly and hand to heart.

☐ Put a smile on your face. Yes, a smile, but if it doesn't come easy, don't force it. Imagine a smile. That'll work for now.

☐ Do absolutely nothing else. Just sit. There's no work assignment here. Just sit and notice how simple, how hard, or anywhere in between the two it is to just sit.

☐ Notice if you start to grade yourself or adjust your seat or breath to make it "right." Just notice.

☐ Continue to turn your attention back to that smile (or the vision of a smile). Hand to belly, hand to heart whenever you feel the urge to bolt or feel like you're forcing anything.

☐ After 10 minutes, gently open your eyes. Take a moment and then, perhaps, jot down anything that comes to mind. For instance, what did it feel like to simply smile with your eyes closed? How did it feel not to do anything, i.e., focus on the breath or walk, etc.?

Live Big Takeaways

☐ Be on the lookout for reminders and "gifts" from the Universe to inspire, and sometimes course correct you, when you're on this Awesome Life journey.

☐ Decide to let the struggle go. Remember, you control your thoughts and reactions to everything and everyone. Choose ease, happiness, and light. Let the Universe catch the drama. It knows exactly how to handle it.

☐ Follow the sound advice of the Potato Chip Lady and tune in with joy to every moment of this life.

Whether it's a subway train you're riding, a book you're reading, a random call from that person you've been thinking about, the Universe is always dropping "Pay attention!" nuggets to wake us to the gift of the present moment. We can get so caught up in what's coming next or daydreaming about our future big wins that we miss the lesson, person, experience right in front of our faces.

Big thanks to the Potato Chip Lady, wherever she is!

11

＊

It's Not a Leap,
It's Just a Step

*"Show up to each moment like
that's all that matters."*

"Get to the end." Until about three years ago, this was my everything statement. I loved it. I loved saying it. I loved the results of it. It was better than
sex. No, not really, but I did really love it.

It worked like a charm, or so I thought, as an executive in corporate America.
It was beautiful for moving people along at a pace I needed. It was fabulous
for ending long, boring, and unnecessary meetings and conversations with my
colleagues and team. It worked with my boyfriends, friends, family, and even
strangers, because everyone would have to hurry up and finish whatever they
were saying or doing that was not as important as what I had to say and do. That
way they could listen to what I thought and focus on me, me, me and my fantastic life and dreams. I loved it. I even thought about having a t-shirt made with
this perfect saying: "Get to the end."

Then I met Bruce Almighty. He was this amazing, intelligent, charming,
thoughtful, ridiculously handsome king who loved to tell stories and take his
sweet time "getting to the end." "Oh Lawd, would you please hurry up already,
oh wonderful love of my life," I would think some of the time. Well, no. Every
time, I would blurt out, "Get to the end!" He would often ignore it and continue
whatever story he was telling. Then one day, he politely said to me, "Relax. I'm

getting there. Why are you always in such a hurry?" It was then that I realized, looking into the sensational face of my favorite guy, that I had been trying to leap through life to "get to the end" for a long time. My goal had not been the journey. It was all about the leap to the other side of that rainbow to get my big ol' shimmery pot of gold. Never mind those silly vibrant colors and intriguing Leprechaun tales along the way. I was all about "Get to the end" or, as I like to call it now, the Big Leap mentality.

The Big Leap mentality is the manifestation of "Get to the end" impatient out-bursts. It's when you've become completely indifferent to the present moment. You couldn't care less about who or what is directly in front of you. You're miss-ing all the micro, amazing bits of life happening at the moment, because all you can see is the big win.

I'd completely bought into the idea of a shortcut to achieving and receiving all I had dreamed on my fancy Vision Board. Snore! Time to drop it.

This Amazing Life journey is a breath-by-breath, step-by-step, win-by-win, fall-by-fall, restart-by-restart deal. Let me be clear here because we're friends and I love you. It's not about and has never been about getting to any end.

Each step that you take lights up your life and inspires the lives of the others you love and serve.

It's in all those colors of the rainbow and whatever the heck that Leprechaun is up to, not in that pot of gold at the end. The pot is empty, love. The gold is hang-ing on the rainbow—the journey!

That said, the silly ego is head-over-heels in love with the "Get to the end" mind-set and thrilled when you latch onto it and ride it like a champ. It makes you be-lieve that you're all powerful: "I'm in control of everything and everybody." You start to buy into the illusion you're getting results faster and better than if you would have just relaxed and listened to the whole story. The ego is a genius con artist. You might want to steer clear of all its lies if you're blazing towards the biggest, boldest life you can imagine. Also, don't forget: when we're swept away with the Big Leap mentality, we begin to buy into *doubt's* song and dance. We get overwhelmed and discouraged when we fall flat on our faces or things don't go as planned. Even when we fly, the thrill is short-lived. You fall right back into the anxiety of how you'll make that next Big Leap happen. Sound familiar?

It's time to shake the "Get to the end" mindset and start living in each moment, each step. That's how you'll stay jazzed on your path. Leaps happen, but don't get it twisted: they come from you consistently showing up, practicing "as if," breathing big, gleefully accepting the support of your pom poms up cheering section, letting go of what does not serve, and making space for the good stuff to come in.

So, basically:

Little steps lead to big leaps.

Here's how I'm actively kicking the "Get to the end" nuttiness. Note the actively, because my Gemini Type A, minus-the-yogini mind loves to hang out with the ego.

- Remember, letting go of old habits, attitudes, and things that don't serve doesn't always come instantly. Stay with your practice and restart when needed.

- Ask others to keep you honest! Tap a close friend or your own Bruce Almighty/spouse/partner/child to call you out whenever you go there. It's like getting a loving little kiss of shock back to what matters—this step, this moment, this right now.

- Celebrate the itty bitty little wins. This is so important, love! It's how you'll stay motivated, inspired, and feeling like you're already taking those Big Leaps.

- Revisit your Vision Board and Roadmap. Laser-focus on what you want and know that it's available and on its way. In the meantime, enjoy the vibrant colors of the rainbow of your life that's happening right now.

We're in this together, and I know how enticing it is to dream of the finish line: a winner with arms up, while someone puts a chunky, blingy medal around your neck and hands you a bagel, apple, water bottle, and salt packet. I get it. But don't forget you had to run that whole race. One mile at a time.

Breathe Big Practice

☐ Time to take that easy seat, hand to belly, hand to heart. Get focused on each and every breath, each and every inhale and exhale. This is a practice of every single *now*. And, every single *now* is every single breath. It's the step vs the leap.

☐ Keep your eyes open.

☐ Focus on a spot on the ground that's slightly ahead of you.

☐ Now close your eyes. Take a deep inhale and exhale. Keep that spot on the ground, that piece of hair, rubber band, or whatever caught your attention in your mind's eye. That's your focus. Your right now.

☐ Each time your mind wanders to a place that doesn't serve the present moment, gently draw your attention back to that spot. No judgment allowed. Just a gentle nudge back.

☐ Keep breathing. Keep coming back to that spot whenever you drift away. Keep watching the inhale that comes and the exhale that goes. And, keep drawing your attention back to that spot.

☐ Take as much time in this practice as you like. It all counts.

I've figured out that leaps don't really exist. I'm sharing the great news with you because we are keeping it real, right? Stay present in the first step, the next, and the next. You'll get there. In fact, you're already there. Surprise!

Live Big Takeaways

☐ Time to drop the Get to the end mindset.

☐ Pay attention to the little steps you make every day. Celebrate them!

☐ Little steps lead to Big Leaps.

There's no need to rush. I'm still learning that. All you want and need is right here in this moment, even if this moment is uncomfortable, painful, or a bit scary. There's something in it that's valuable. There's something there that will help support your journey. Make sure to make yourself available to hear it, see it, and experience it.

12

Grab Your Superhero Powerful God / Goddess Cape

"Trust and see yourself as the Superstar that others do. Know that the moment is yours if you choose."

After reading Shonda Rhimes's *The Year of Yes*, I started getting out of the shower every day, butt naked, hands on hips, doing my Wonder Woman stance in the mirror. If you've read the book, you totally get it. If you've ever seen Wonder Woman, you totally get it. If not, here's the gist: you're a superhero. Time to reclaim your power.

I bought the book after a happily challenged year of retreats, workshops, classes, and personal difficulties that left me completely beat and walking around on empty. Funny, I actually thought the book was about not saying "yes"—meaning, I thought it was a guide to saying "no," written by a genius writer and goddess of television. Regardless, I loved it. That said, what resonated with me most was the reminder of the Wonder Woman inside me.

Don't you know that you're powerfully divine?

Growing up, I loved watching Wonder Woman on television. I watched *The Secrets of Isis*, too, because she was Egyptian and had an amulet, and I thought that was cool. But, Wonder Woman spun and lassoed dudes and stuff, so it was a tie. Regardless, they both rocked. And I wanted to be like them: strong, fearless, and ready to kick ass, if required.

Back to the butt-naked-out-of-the-shower thing. In her book, Shonda talks about being incredibly shy and lacking the confidence to deal with a lot of social situations that come with being a rising star. She goes on to share the tactics she uses to challenge that part of herself to say "yes" to everything for an entire year. One of her tactics is the Wonder Woman stance, where you stand in front of the mirror, hands on hips, puff up your chest, chin up, and conjure your power from within. So, of course, I had to try it. And, guess what? It worked!

It was a tough time. I had way too much going on and not enough focus or clarity around what truly mattered. My mind's Vision Board had become a blurry mess, to say the least. It happens when you're sleep deprived, running around trying "To Do" all things and be all things to all people. Snore.

Yep, I was mentally and emotionally tapped out. Enter Shonda's Wonder Woman stance. Along with Bruce Almighty, my yoga practice, breathwork, lovin' folks, massages, and facials with Christine, I added the butt-naked-Wonder-Woman stance to my daily Awesome Life journey practice. Just one to five minutes of it did the trick. Ready to rock!

Unfortunately, you may not have your lover, family, friends, and Rockstar Peeps around you 24/7 to constantly pom poms up when you really need it. And, that's a good thing because this journey is about you draping on your own superhero cape, belt, or cool gold amulet every day—all by your powerfully divine self.

What would you do if you knew you could fly? Well, you can, so time to get your soar on. You were born to fly and do whatever the heck it is you want to do that serves you, your family, friends, and others. Now, it's about polishing and exercising those wings. They've gotten a bit dusty over the years with all that doubt, fear, stress, no purpose, no vision, no plan, negative thinking nonsense. I know, remember I'm on the journey, too. I understand how you can start to believe it's easier and safer to stay grounded and all plain-Jane-same as everybody else. Soaring to new heights at work, finally starting your own business, traveling the world to exotic places, launching that cool new app, asking that guy out, or donating time and loads of money to serve people just can't work for you. Man! That ego is good at its job, right?

Here's what I want you to do. Grab a piece of paper or your journal. Set your phone or kitchen timer (or just watch the clock) for five minutes. In that time, I want you to write down your life's "Superhero Moments." These are all the times you've ever thought or (like me) said out loud one of those you-handled-your-business statements, like "Oh hell yes!" or "I'm the bomb!" or "I rocked that!"

Your list might look a little something like this:

- Got an A on that crazy hard statistics exam
- Finished two marathons
- Got the kids off to school today, then got to work on time, fully dressed, and crushed that meeting with the execs
- Picked up kids from school on time, made dinner, and got a full night's sleep
- Stood at the top of Machu Picchu
- Got into a headstand in yoga class
- Kissed that special girl
- Kissed that special guy
- Sang "This Girl Is on Fire" at karaoke and won the contest
- Good hair day
- Finally signed up for that Tae Kwon Do class

Catch my drift?

Take this time. Right the moments down. This is you tapping into the greatness within you. And if you're struggling to come up with one thing, do the exercise with your love, family, or friends. Ask them about your "Superhero Moments" and get ready because:

The people who really love you see you. They know your light. They've been paying attention, even when you haven't.

This list is the one you'll need when you start to self-sabotage, hold your breath, or get knocked off your path. I always think about my favorite television super-heroines who were smart, resourceful, and constantly learning about all the evil out there trying to take over the world. They were always adjusting their suits and gear to meet the challenge of the day—like a boss.

Take a look at your list. Think about the work, dedication, practice, detours, and falls that happened before you got to that "I'm the bomb!" state. Meditate on that for a minute, superhero. You did it, and you'll do it again and again as we walk this Awesome Life together. Got my lasso and amulet. Let's get it!

As you start or restart each second, moment, or day (whatever it takes!) rededi-cating yourself to your purpose, gazing at your Vision Board, and revisiting your focused, straightforward, simple Roadmap, use this list to remind yourself of all your past wins, from small to gigantic. You've accomplished, given, and shared so much already, love. You've got to take the next step on this journey. You were born to fly!

Breathe Big Practice

☐ Take an easy seat and close your eyes.

☐ Here's a change up! Take both hands to rest palms down on your knees or thighs. We're getting grounded in this exercise. It's time to tap into all that superhero power that lies in the very foundation of you.

☐ Take a breath in through your nose and exhale through your mouth. I dare you to stick out your tongue and make a sound. Maybe a bit of a roar? Go for it!

☐ Continue for as long as you like and see if you can extend the inhale and the exhale.

Don't be surprised if this breathwork leaves you feeling a bit wound up. That's the idea! Let's fly!

Live Big Takeaways

☐ You were born a superhero; just dust off your cape and practice flying again.

☐ Do your "Superhero Moments" exercise by yourself or with friends. It will help to remind you that, ummm, you're a Rockstar and you've claimed so many victories in the past for yourself and others.

☐ Rededicate yourself to knowing and living in your power. You're too amazing not to shine.

When you get reacquainted with your superhero self and start standing, hands on hips, feeling your divine power, you'll actually start to believe that nothing can hold you back or down for long. And you're going to need this belief, because the ups and the downs, the highs and lows will come. You see, this guide isn't about teaching you how to prevent "stuff" from happening, it's all about being able to tap into that power when shit hits the fan. And it will.

13

Keep Breathing. Stuff Changes

"Inhale, Exhale, Onward!"

My BFF Betsy and I call it the "Wall Slide." What is the Wall Slide, you ask? Have you ever watched a soap opera or melodrama where some traumatic, life-changing event happens and the main character backs into a wall, screams with tears, and proceeds to slide down the wall into an inconsolable puddle of hot messness? You have witnessed, ladies and gentlemen, the Wall Slide.

Public service announcement: inevitably, you will slam head first into many emotional, mental, and physical walls on this Awesome Life journey. I know I have. I've got a list of dented walls and pool-sized puddles so long that it's impossible to list them all. But, here are a few for the ages:

- Spiraling into the depths of darkness in a non-loving, going-nowhere-fast relationship until finally the Slide equals a week of hysterical sobbing on the cold bathroom tile in dirty sweat pants and my 2000 Honolulu Marathon Finisher t-shirt.

- Running myself so mentally and physically ragged with worry over not having enough money to pay my bills and checking every damn thing off the To Do list that I ended up in the hospital with viral meningitis—10 times! That's 10 separate Wall Slides. Not winning.

- My handsome, light-of-my-family's-life teenage brother Devon died in a car accident on his way back from his first few weeks in college.

No party here, to say the least. As a matter of fact, some of these Walls are downright vicious.

When my brother died, my family was wounded. No, that's not right. That's not right at all. In fact, we were completely devastated. There are no other words. And yet, we went on. We conjured our superhero capes, lassos, and amulets. We puffed up and dusted off our wings. We refocused on our purpose, vision, and faith that there's absolutely something greater for all of us and that there's meaning and a big ol' light even in our darkest hour. We embraced the "nothing can hold me back" shining-star energy of my brother that radiated through all of us. The Wall was no match for that.

You are brighter than any obstacle. Walk on.

Any Wall Slide you've found yourself in is just the Universe's wake-up call. It's the start or the restart button that's being pushed for you because you've probably been walking around playing tiddlywinks with a boring, mediocre, sub-fabulous life, or, even worse, an unintentional, anti-Rockstar, loveless, non-serving life. Nothing to see here. Snore.

For me, my brother's death was one of the biggest wake-up calls of my life, if not the biggest. Everything immediately became more vibrant, urgent, and "today's all you've got so what you gonna do with it, sweets" real. What the hell was I doing with my life? Was I rocking it like I meant it and serving all I could, or was I just puttering along like I had 100 more years to get it in? I not only owed it to Devon, I owed it to the powerfully divine in me and to the world to show up as my most sensational self. Ummm, right now!

The Wall Slide moments are, at the least, uncomfortable, and at the most, mind-blowingly painful. Pain is a sign from the Universe to stop, drop, rest, get quiet, heal, be loved, and ask for guidance on the next steps. However, I see discomfort as the "Go" sign for change. It's that nagging little thing that makes you squirm or catches your breath until you switch positions. Or, when it gets cold and you grab a sweater or blanket to warm up. Or, when you sense layoffs are coming at work, but no one's talking. Discomfort is, for me, a happy alarm before you slip into that Wall Slide of pain. It may be telling you it's time to learn something new, meet someone new, or go some place new.

If you're really feelin' this Awesome Life stuff, you'll start to welcome that alarm and see it for what it is. It's your chance to dive into your big, powerfully divine, superhero, purpose-driven breath and take action that falls right in line with the fancy Vision Board and Roadmap you've crafted.

Discomfort is a good thing. Get uncomfortable. It means your life, your abundance, your light is about to expand.

What I continue to learn and share is that, yep, life can get big-time ugly sometimes before it gets better. Transforming crappy into Awesome is not for the meek. Insert superhero mindset here. I told you when you started or restarted this that it would take guts and dedication and walking with *doubt* still knowing that you are worthy. You hear me?! You are worthy!

When you're going through it:

- **Practice gratitude**. It's easy to be all pom poms up, happy-go-lucky, kissy face when things seem to be going your way. It's when you hit the Wall that you can sometimes forget the magic words "Thank you." You can start to pick apart or ignore the wonderful people and things that are already in your life. Take a moment in your daily stillness (because I know that you've been practicing!). Focus on what, who, and the circumstances in your life today that are light, bright, and glowing. They are there. You just have to want to see them and celebrate them.

- **Show your Vision Board some love.** First, if you haven't already, make sure you can see it regularly. It is the change you wish to see in your life. So, ummm, see it! Take some time to revisit your goals and dreams. Grab your glue stick, tape, and add, delete, or reorganize. Get all cozy with it again. Get revved up and in the "You've got this!" state of mind.

- **Phone a friend.** You are never alone and those who love you and support your vision and dreams want to help. They want to listen. They want to give you that virtual hug you need. They will do their best to help pick you up out of your puddle of hot messness, give hugs, laugh with you, clean you up, and encourage you to ease on down your Roadmap once again.

- **Get still.** Yes, we're back here again. It's the key, ya'll! The answers, the healing, the next right action is in the quiet space. So, sit down, let go, and let in.

What I do love about a good Wall Slide (and yes, there's more to love) is the stripping away of pretense. You can't put concealer and lipstick on it and hope that no one sees your pain, your failures, or your missteps oozing off of you. You hit that Wall for a reason. So, leave the stuff that doesn't serve you "on the mat", as I say in my yoga classes and workshops. When you get up (and you will get up out of that puddle), what wants to fly is the real you that's been aching to take a hold of this journey.

Breathe Big Practice

- ☐ If you've found yourself always doing your Breathe Big practice in the same place and at the same time, change it up! Be the change you wish to see. Find another space in your home, office, or wherever. And, instead of right before bed, try this first thing in the morning or the middle of the day.

- ☐ Find an easy seat. Close your eyes. Take hand to belly and hand to heart. Take some time to just watch and listen to the breath flow in and out of your body.

- ☐ After a moment, start to pay attention to just your inhale. Notice how each time you take a breath in, it changes. It might be bigger, longer, shorter, louder, or softer. Just allow and watch it flow. In time, switch up to your exhale. Notice with each moment that passes how your breath changes its rhythm (or YOU change the rhythm and notice how you feel with each change).

- ☐ Spend a few minutes in stillness and then let it go.

If anything, this exercise helps me to stay present and "ride the wave" of my breath without freaking out. It really helps me understand that regardless of what comes, I'm still okay. As a matter of fact, I'm in control of it. I just take a deeper or shorter breath the next time, or hold the breath in or out a little longer, or whatever helps me get as clear as I need to roll with or rock whatever I'm living through at that moment.

Remember, you've got this! Keep breathing. Stuff really does change, because you can change it!

Live Big Takeaways

☐ The Wall Slide is your wake-up call. Pay attention to how you got to that place. Get up. Learn from your mistakes. Polish your light. Set a new direction and keep going!

☐ Being uncomfortable ain't so bad! Read the warning signs that discomfort brings. It might be time for you to get still. So, get quiet and ask for help and guidance. You might be going the wrong way or need to be better prepared for the way you are going.

☐ You are the maker of your Awesome Life. Heads up! You are the driver on this journey. Own the changes you can and decide to make those changes light up your path. As for the rest, let them go. Breathe, love, and fly with what you can control. Let the Universe handle the rest. The Universe is so much better at this stuff than we are.

So, what's the point? Well, Wall Slides will happen on this journey or else it wouldn't be life. I wish I could tell you different, but that's just not real. It's how you show up in that Wall Slide moment that counts. Will you take the ride, release what no longer serves, learn, get up, restart, and fly? Will you see that you already have what you need to move forward and shine, Rockstar?

14

※

It's Not Magic.
You're Magic.

*"The Awesome comes
from the inside."*

My marketing coach and friend Gwenna Lucas suggested that as I revisited my business plan and Roadmap for the year, I interview three to five of my most engaged yoga and wellness clients. These were the people who consistently attended my talks, classes, workshops, webinars, retreats—and just overall supported my mission to serve. All of them are Rockstar Peeps for sure! I asked them all a few basic questions, but I started each interview with this: Why me? I needed to get to the bottom of why these amazing people chose me and kept choosing me, my practice, my services, and my offering as their go-to power-house.

I was surprised that as I met with each individually, they all answered the "Why me?" question with pretty much the same response: "You are an incredible yoga teacher, no doubt. But I come for the word. For your word. I come to move, breathe, sit, listen, cry, laugh, and connect on the mat. It's your words. It's what you say and how you say it. That's the magic I never want to miss."

Well, alrighty then.

I guess I've always known that I had the gift of gab, although sometimes labeled as a beautiful curse by some family and friends. HA! Who knew that this would be at the center of my service to others? Perfect. I could do this all day long! And for the most part, without wanting to be distracted by social media, coffee breaks, and Bruce Almighty kisses (scratch that, I always want to be distracted by Bruce Almighty kisses), this is a good thing.

But back to my revelation: how awesome is it that it didn't take a full-on Wall Slide into hot-messness to realize the depth of my power? That is, to see, or to be reminded I was the unicorn, the fairy, the genie in the bottle; that this voice I was born with was one of my greatest gifts to the world. Whoa! Get out of here! Me? All the bazillion things I'd tried to share really boiled down to one thing: me! Pom poms up, I guess?

It's one thing to have the light bulb turn on. It's another to live in that light and rock it. *Doubt* and *little fear* would just have you hang out in the dark, twiddling their thumbs while you forget about that magic wand you've got in your back pocket, when action is required.

Time to revamp your purpose statement, that daily To Thrive list, your Vision Board, and your Roadmap based on your magic. Everything else will just lead to: same ol' same ol', been there done that, broke as no joke, single and not loving it, hate my job and my life. Snore.

Here's what happens when I decide to ride the wave of my inner magician: I'm writing and publishing this book after three years of saying I would. I'm booking motivational speaking engagements. I'm giving inspirational talks around the globe. I'm letting my magic—my voice—light up and serve others.

What are you doing? What is your magic? What is your power? How do you connect or reconnect to it? How do you use it in service to yourself and others? Well, if you don't know or aren't sure, you've got some homework to do, love. All the good stuff on this Awesome Life journey comes from that mojo you were born with, superstar.

Listen, I totally get it.

Sometimes what we think is our magic can turn out to be a dud or lead us right to that Wall.

So how do you know that you know that you know?

- **Ask the Universe.** Okay, time to get all hugged up with the Universe, God, or whatever you call your highest source of light and just ask for what you need: "What's my magic?" "Please show me how I can serve?" "How do

I light up my life and the lives of others?" "Show me a sign because I'm clueless." Then get still. Listen and watch for the answers.

- **Ask your friends, family, students, clients, etc.** Just like I did! Those who have experienced your most magical self definitely want to see and feel more of it. I've found that they're happy to have a chat and share. Remember, they want to help you shine!

- **Make a list of everything you love to do.** Yes, your magic lies in those things that you could do all day long without watching the clock. List everything on a blank sheet of paper. I'm talking hobbies, travel, business, walking dogs, or whatever makes you tingle a little bit or a lot when you think of it.

- **Do an experiment or two.** Take a day (yes, a whole day!) and just do that thing you love. Notice how you feel, how you look, how the people around you seem to feel. Could this be it?

- **Take a risk or two.** So, what if you're not completely sure? Take action and see where it takes you. You won't know until you try. And, if it fizzles out or you're picking yourself up from another Wall Slide—restart.

How committed to this Awesome Life journey are you? Stop and ask yourself right now. If you're all in, you're way past due to start using your real power, doing the things you love to rise up and sparkle.

It's you. It's always been you. It will always be you. And this, oh fabulous one, is the best news of the day. You get to write or rewrite your story anytime you want. You get to wave your wand and love, give, and receive a little or a lot more of whatever you want, whenever you want.

Breathe Big Practice

Here's what you'll need:
"Things you love to do" list
A pen/pencil and paper or journal

☐ Grab that list of "Things you love to do" and find an easy seat. Get still. Close your eyes.

☐ Take hand to belly, hand to heart. Breathe. Just allow the breath to come and go.

☐ Take a few moments sitting with your list and your breath.

☐ Ask the questions "What is my power?" "How do I serve?" "Show me the way."

☐ Each time you find yourself distracted or allowing your thoughts to run away with you, just ask the questions. Keep coming back to the breath.

☐ Spend a few minutes (or more) in your seat. Then gently release the questions and the breath.

☐ Take some time to write down any thoughts or images you may have experienced. Take note of anything that makes you think, "That's it!" Circle and highlight those things and then take action. Just a little step counts.

Live Big Takeaways

☐ It's you. You're the magic, the power that will rock this journey in the direction you want and the one that serves others.

☐ Get reconnected to your magic by asking the Universe, your friends, your family, your clients. Ask the questions!

☐ Take action based on what you really love. Do the things that make you feel alive. That's your magic! Let *doubt* and *little fear* come along for the ride, but keep it moving.

It's so much easier to believe that whatever will change the course of your life is outside of you. False! Happy to say that it's all you, baby. It's on the inside. You have what you need. Tap into it. Even when it feels hopeless or hard. Get still. Let go of whatever nonsense *little fear*, *doubt*, and their cronies are screaming from the back seat. Listen to your higher source. Ask for direction. Then let it rock!

15

Your New Mantra:
I Deserve It!

"Who me?.
Yes, me!."

When I was young, I was convinced my oldest brother was a conceited, pompous jerk. In those days, he was popular and I was not. He was funny, while I was ever so serious and intense. He was a charming teenager; I was an awkward preteen. He was confident; I was playing confident. So basically, he was awesome sauce and I had no sauce. Anyhoot, he would always say, conceitedly, "If I don't love me, who will?" and then run off with his friends to hang out with girls, or go to parties, or do really cool things you do when you're a teen. Ugh! It annoyed me how "I'm so fine" into himself he was. But I loved and adored him. He was my Rockstar confident hero as a preteen. Actually, I'm not sure he even knows that. So, to my brother, insert the "Did you ever know that you're my hero" song here. Love you!

There's this thing about walking and dancing around like you're the bomb-diggity and the world is your oyster: The Universe starts to dance along with you. As a matter of fact, it turns up the volume to full-on rave with you! It gets super-geeked that you've tapped into your magic, sprouted your golden wings, and started soaring through this journey like somebody's hooking you up minute by minute with all you could ever imagine. It's this absurd notion that you actually, oh, I don't know deserve this Awesome Life. What? Get out of here with that crazy talk, you say? Yeah, say it with me: I deserve it!

Did you just flinch? Did your ego scream right in your face, "Selfish!"? Have you ever thought that what's really holding you back is that you can't wrap your head, heart, and soul around the fact, the absolute fact, that you deserve every single ounce of joy, love, abundance, and light to infinity? Hello! This is me screaming from the rooftops: "You deserve it!" But I can't be the believer for you. This is your path. This is your story. Now, what load of crap are you feeding yourself and others? That's the real question.

Yes, thank you, and I'll have more of that, please.

Whatever you think you deserve from the Universe is what you'll get. Period. That's all, folks. No thought, feeling, or action goes unheard, unfelt, or unseen. It's all energy. And you get to determine if it's energy focused on your purpose, your Vision, your Roadmap, or if it's "No thank you, I'm not good enough. Pass! Give it to Beyoncé and Jay Z." Sound ridiculous? Yeah, because it is. It's absolutely nuts. You are divine. You're like the biggest Rockstar ever, and you deserve it!

But how do you let go of the past and future to indulge wholeheartedly in the joy of this moment, this today you've created and deserve? That's your dilemma, right? I know, because I'm totally on this journey with you, and I get it. It's so easy to dwell on our past royal screw-ups, because it has somehow become sexier to dramatize our foolishness. The list is long and gloriously ripe with hot-messness. I know! I'm living this with you, baby. Been there, done that.

The past is done. The future is none of our business. Today's the party.

How do you write your "Oh hell yes, I deserve all of it!" story and live it on a daily basis? If this is about starting or restarting this Awesome Life journey, it's time to look at your life with a new set of eyes.

- Who are you now? (as you're taking real steps to rock this Awesome Life journey)
- Who do you want to be? (Ahem … Vision Board!)
- What do you want to create?
- Who do you want to serve? (Hello! Purpose statement!)
- Where do you want to go on this journey, and who do you want to go with you? (Insert Roadmap happy dance here!)

It's so easy to talk about who you were back in the day, with a highlight of all your Oscar-winning Wall Slides, failures, and not-so-Awesome living. The ego, *doubt*, and *little fear* love to hang out with a big buttery bowl of popcorn and tell those tales. Good times! Not. Snore. But if you keep telling that story, you'll keep believing that story, and you'll keep living that story. I did. I get it. Totally un-fun. So, change your words.

Words are powerful. Use them wisely.

Think about the words and phrases you use on a daily basis. Think about them. How often are they positive, uplifting, ready-for-the-party types of thoughts and words? Statistics say that over 80% of thoughts we have each day are negative. That's only 20% Awesome Life "I'm a superhero" thoughts. Snore.

I'm constantly at work editing my thoughts and words. When you actually start to analyze the craziness that you think and say about yourself, others, and situations, it's wild! A few of my everyday favorites, plus my edits include:

I'm fat. — I'm fabulous and sexy.

It's hard to do. — I can do anything I want because the Universe is on my side.

I'm old. — See "I'm fabulous and sexy" above.

I don't have any money. — I'm wealthy and money's always flowing to me.

I failed. — Whew! So, happy I showed up, did my best, and learned. Next?

One of the saddest things for me to hear from people is that they don't believe they deserve greatness. And I hear it with these types of words and phrases every day from family, friends, and strangers. It just makes my soul ache. I see you. I see your fabulousness. I see you doing the work and getting in shape. I see you getting still and asking for guidance. And I absolutely, with or without a doubt, know that what you dream is wrapped with a big bow and waiting for you to call its name. You deserve it. You just have to get your mind right, baby!

Where are your Rockstar Peeps who, like my big brother, talk, walk, and party like this fabulous life was made just for them? Keeping in mind that their "fabulous life" is whatever they've personally envisioned, what kinds of things do you hear them saying all the time? Check out the way they stand and move. Who are the people they hang out with? A bunch of Negative Nellies or the I-Deserve-It-Bunch? What about them says, "Bring it to me! I'm ready, willing, and available to rock it"?

When you think it, say it, and practice it, you'll start to believe it. And then it's on!

"A mantra is a word or phrase that is repeated often or that expresses someone's basic beliefs," says Wikipedia. It's an affirmation, and if you know me, you know how I love my affirmations! I wake up each morning and speak them out loud. Throughout the day, I'm whispering them quietly or repeating them in my head as I happily go about my business. I blurt them out randomly to Bruce Almighty and his daughter. I post them on the master-bathroom mirror—that is, if I haven't already written them in red lipstick. Note: The red lipstick sometimes freaks me (and Bruce Almighty) out in the middle of the night, so you might want to stick with post-it notes.

Hear me now, amazing one! This whole deserving thing has to be a part of your daily practice. Remember, the Universe is watching, listening, and waiting for you to put on your crown and receive what is yours. And if you don't want to love, Live Big, and share it all, the Universe is like "Cool. I'll bounce it right over here to your neighbor. Not a problem. Smooches!" I know you hear me because you've seen it happen. I've seen it happen. It's those times when you've been all in your head about why you're such a bad person, or you didn't do enough of this or that, or how it's okay that your best friend hits the lottery, because you're not ready. Seriously, as you're lost in your 80% negativity, your best friend or the guy at work wins a trip to Hawaii or gets that promotion that had your name written all over it.

The mantra, the phrase, "I deserve it," is one half of your practice. The other half? "Thank you." No questions asked. Just "Thank you." When the Universe delivers, a simple "Thank you" will do. That whole second-guessing game? "Are these flowers for me?" or "Maybe there's been a mistake and this check with my name and social security number on it was sent to the wrong person." It's for the birds. Certainly not for the I-Deserve-It-Bunch who are the bosses of their Awesome Life and journey.

Breathe Big Practice

☐ Time to practice! Grab your Vision Board. Remember that you set the time on these breathing exercises. It's your practice. You can sit for one minute or one hour. It all counts.

☐ Find an easy seat and just take a moment with your Vision Board. Take it all in.

☐ Then close your eyes. Take a deep breath in and exhale through your mouth.

☐ Say "I deserve it" three times out loud.

☐ Then take another deep breath in and exhale through your mouth.

☐ Get still. Take hand to belly and hand to heart. Just allow your thoughts to come and go. No judgment. Just breathe.

☐ Sit for as long as you want. When you're ready, gently open eyes to your Vision Board and repeat "I deserve it" three times and "Thank you" once.

It's a powerful experience when you begin to realize that you're worthy and that all that you dream is available to you. You deserve it.

Live Big Takeaways

☐ When you believe you deserve it, the Universe gets on board with your party.

☐ Thoughts and words are powerful. Time to raise your percentage of positive thoughts to 100%.

☐ Find your Rockstar Peeps, the I-Deserve-It-Bunch, and cozy up to whatever they're doing that's brightening their lives and the lives of others. They get it.

☐ Practice your "I deserve it" mantra or affirmation daily, all day, out loud or to yourself.

☐ Gratitude is everything. A simple "Thank you" goes a long way for allowing more of the good that you got in your life.

16

Fear Doesn't Get a Voice Today

"You were born fearless. Nothing has changed. Roar."

In honor of my New Year's resolutions in 2014, I wrote this ditty to *little fear*:

> This year it's all about walking right through that crazy, mind-blowing, deafening, stop-you-in-your-tracks, monster of a thing called Fear. It's a year of stepping right into my light and leaving behind whatever it is that holds me back from sharing my passions and gifts. Fear is a lie. I say it all of the time, but haven't truly lived the words. So, this year, I'm putting it all on the table, calling myself to the carpet, a come to whatever deity you so choose moment. Time's up, Fear! I'm putting you in lowercase, dressing you in raggedy clothes, wiping off your red lipstick (Wait that's MY red lipstick you thief!), snatching and destroying your fancy "You can't do it!" pom poms up, blowing away the purple haze you so love to use to cover the light, joy, love, and all things, people, places sensational that are waiting for me. Oh, and don't you dare try to cloak yourself in Worry, Stress, Laziness, Guilt, and the rest because I'm totally hip and they've also been cut from the chorus line. So, basically, *little fear*—you're fired. Thanks for coming, now hit the bricks! My time to shine!

I'd had enough. I was done. I was over it. I was ... well, I was scared out of my mind! I was starting to freak out with all the amazing and not-so-amazing things I had dreamed, planned, and manifested in my life. So, my big, badass letter, which I shared with the world on my blog and newsletter and with friends and family, was a public manifestation of me being scared crapless and totally faking it 'til I made it. Otherwise known as Rockstar Awesome Life golden rule:

Do it scared.

There's a whole bunch of everything out there written on *little fear* and how it can drive us, freak us out, or even completely incapacitate us. I'm of the school that *little fear* is not my friend. I'm not talking about the there's a bear-about-to-eat-your-face off fear. Umm, that's real and you should run! I'm talking about *doubt's* cousin, *little fear*. Yeah, not my friend. That said, after my own thorough investigation and experimentation, living my life, I've become cordial with the enemy. I get *little fear*. I focus on seeing it for what it truly is. When it screams for attention, I often let it come along for the ride, on mute in the back seat. I guess I can say that *little fear* is good to have around from time to time to remind me of just how off-the-charts fearless I've become on this Awesome Life journey. You see, if *little fear* shows up, it's often because something new and incredible—something I've asked for or haven't even asked for yet—is knocking on my door. What's knocking is more than likely something or someone that *little fear* would like to point out that I have no business with because I'll make a fool of myself or end up in a head-first Wall Slide.

But, *little fear* doesn't come out of nowhere. Keep in mind that I'm not a psychologist or therapist, but I think that we do the *little fear* rain dance when we know in our heart of hearts that the next little step will be a big leap that rocks our journey and leaves us wide open. "Oh please *little fear* come save me from myself! I'm about to be fabulous!" And that might mean having to let go of something, someone, some place, some drama, some good stuff. But I'm sure I'm just talking about me, right? Snore.

Just say, "Yes!" It freaks little fear out.

How powerful is the word "yes"? Super-hero powerful! Boom! It changes things. It's the head cheerleader, lead singer, and CEO of growth and Awesome Life journeys. It's the new black. Let's put that on t-shirt! "'Yes' is the new black!" I love it!

Let's play the "yes" game, shall we? How many times today have you said "yes"? Now, think about it. How many times have you said "no"? I play with this all the time. Sometimes I wake up and say, "I'm going to say 'yes' to everything today!"

And, inevitably, something really cool comes of it, whether for myself or in service of others. To be honest, sometimes it sucks—like jumping off a 30-foot cliff in Jamaica into the ocean and busting my tailbone. True story, and it was painful and not recommended. Oh well. Next "yes," please.

There's definitely a time and a place for "no." I just encourage you to check in with your Awesome Life superhero Rockstar self before you go there to make sure it comes from your most authentic place and not with *little fear* driving the car. "No" is a learned, robotic response when you're not being the boss of your life. Just as you've learned it, you can drop it, as necessary, with intention and practice.

You've already said "yes" to start or restart this Awesome Life journey with your purpose, your Vision Board, your Roadmap, you're letting go and letting in, and your getting back up after dramatic Wall Slides. What's stopping you now? Not-so-friendly *little fear* is happy to hang around, distract, and taunt you with all its gruesome "could happen," "might fail," and "probably will be laughed at" threats. The moment is yours. You can give in to the ridiculous notion of *little fear* or you could flow through it and know that, with or without a doubt, the Universe is conspiring to support you and *little fear* doesn't stand a chance against your powerfully divine self! Which do you choose? Because, it is a choice. The Awesome Life "I Deserve It Bunch" are all about the "yes" and throwing shade at *little fear* and you're on the team. So, help *little fear* to the back seat, give it a juice box, animal cookies, and get to the "yes" part of your life. And, yes, it is that easy.

Try turning your "No" moments into "Yes!" this year and see what happens.

Take mental (or perhaps written) note of how often your mind goes to the "no" place in one day and possible reasons for that. Write down all the times that "yes!" has changed your life or the lives of others in a positive way.

Maybe it's the Gemini Yogini Type A in me, but I'm always thinking that I'll miss out on the experience of a lifetime if I let *little fear* keep me from doing something. So, most of the time, I just go for it. I just jump. But only you know your journey. Only you know (and you know!) when *little fear* is driving you or when you are showing up bold and magnificent to your life's purpose.

Breathe Big Practice

☐ Find an easy seat. Get still. Close your eyes.

☐ Place both hands onto your belly this time. Ever notice how when you're scared your stomach hurts? Yep, lots of energy runs through our tummies. So, let's focus here.

☐ Breathe in and breathe out. Feel your belly rise and fall.

☐ Play with closing your mouth and try breathing just through your nose.

☐ Spend a moment or as long as you like in your seat.

Live Big Takeaways

☐ Remember, little fear only has the power you give it.

☐ Practice saying "Yes!" and see where that takes you on your journey.

☐ Do it scared.

You've come this far knowing your most Awesome Life is yours. Keep going! Walking with *little fear* is just another step in your journey. But it's a big step. I know! I was super-scared for way too long. What a relief to put *little fear* in its place! You're starting to clean house of the crap that's been freaking you out and holding you back from doing your thing. Stay the course. Keep looking at the stuff that doesn't serve and making space for abundance.

17

Empty Wallet Syndrome Doesn't Serve

"It's zero fun being broke.
It helps no one.
It's not your destiny."

Before I took the leap out of corporate America and jumped headfirst into teaching yoga, I had starlit, romantic dreams of walking around in yoga pants and bare feet all day, sharing this amazing practice with packed classes of loving yogis in a gorgeous, light-filled studio that smelled of nag champa incense, taking loungey, free-time afternoon walks in Central Park, while drinking coconut water, and planning my next trip to Bali to teach yoga on the beach in a bikini. And, of course, I would get paid like a champ to do all of this.

This did not happen. Instead, I was teaching one class in a dimly lit room with tape and wood over the windows to secure the air conditioners. Having exhausted my savings, my bank account was in the red. I was in debt, counting pennies to buy a subway card, and barely paying my rent. Sexy, right? Not. Snore.

I wanted to believe in the fantasy, even though I knew better, or at least I thought I knew better. You know the one. That fantasy where if you do what you love, then money rains down on you from the heavens. That's what it looked like on television and social media. And television and social media are real! (Ummm, no, they are not. I repeat, no, they are not.) You don't always hear and see it, but the reality is that you may have one million followers on Instagram, you might be a celebrity yogi or Rockstar motivational speaker and author, and you might be traveling the world in service to others, but you may still have what I like to call EWS—Empty Wallet Syndrome.

Empty Wallet Syndrome is no joke. It's ugly. It hurts. It's crippling. It made me feel like a fraud. There I was, all dressed up in my faux Awesome Lifeness, showing up every day with *little fear* at the wheel, freaked out from creditor calls and threats of eviction. True story. Enter panic attacks. Enter Wall Slides. How could I be so broke after having worked in finance for years, been at the top of my corporate game with a healthy 401k, harboring a pseudo plan for a fledgling business, and having lots of positive energy? How could I literally be eating water crackers for dinner and dodging my landlord?

Here's how: I grew up believing you must work hard and all the time to make money. And, money just comes and goes. Sometimes you have it; sometimes you don't. And, when you have it, you should spend it, all of it on Christmas gifts, travel, or other experiences. Or you worry constantly about losing it. And when you don't have it, you stress out with demons chasing you in your sleep and wake up with cold sweats.

I grew up believing it was perfectly normal to have a dollar in your wallet and enough money in your bank account to keep it open. You just get by. Other people had lots of money, but not me. Oh! And, the Universe would provide. Empty Wallet Syndrome was just a way of life.

My relationship with money sucked, to put it lightly. And, most importantly, it didn't serve me or anyone else. There weren't going to be any retreats to Bali, supporting my family, and donating to charitable organizations. Hell, I was the charity! I had a complete disregard for the power and energy of money.

Money, money, money, money ... MONEY!

It was time to change my relationship with money and see it with brand-new eyes and a brand-new wallet, to boot. That is, if I wanted to ride in the first-class car of life and share that ride with others, I couldn't do it broke. You can't do it broke. It doesn't work that way. Money is energy. That energy fills up the engine so you can ditch the water crackers, call a taxi, and spread your light in bigger, better ways. You need it. And perhaps, like me, you need to change your mind about it.

I held a series of workshops for yoga teachers called *Do the Yoga Hustle: How to really make money teaching yoga so that you can KEEP teaching yoga*. The funny thing is that although people showed up excited and ready to learn, no one wanted to talk about money. Not really. It was taboo. Yogis, scratch that, people don't like to talk about money, right? Money is the root of all evil, right? No, not really. No, not at all.

In my workshops, when I started to talk about money and how much I loved it, wanted it, couldn't get enough of it, wanted them to have loads of it, and how to get it, the yoga teachers all gave me the side eye and probably decided I should be banned from all things yoga and kicked off the Earth. Ha! And a whopping SNORE!

Are you tripped out about money? Does it scare you when you don't have it and when you do have it? If the answer is yes, I totally get it. I'm on this journey with you, and I so know that *little fear* and *doubt* are all over you with this money thing. But I'm learning, and you can too, that getting your head and your wallet right about money takes practice. Sound familiar?

This is a step-by-step process. You didn't create your thoughts, attitudes, and behaviors around money overnight, and you won't change them overnight. And, you don't want to change them overnight. Not if you want lasting change. Who wants to go back to being broke and pitiful? Remember, it doesn't serve your purpose-driven path or anyone else, and it just basically sucks wind.

Got a plan? No? Good luck with that!

Grab a pen and a piece of paper. Let's get you on the right track. I'm with you on this and you deserve it!

Note: If you're already rockin' it like you mean it financially, read on. Ya never know! This journey is long, we hope, and stuff happens, Wall Slides happen, and you might need to get up, restart, rehabilitate from EWS. You can file this chapter under "Break glass in case of emergency."

- **Speak your money demons.** Get it all out, love! What is your money drama? Do you hate it? Do you love it so much it haunts your every thought? Do you completely suck at managing it? Are you afraid of it? Write down your thoughts. Let it be known! This is so important, and it's just for you. Unlike me, you don't have to write a book about it and tell the world. But you definitely need to tell yourself the truth or you're bound to continue on your EWS journey. Unfun.

- **Get real with your current situation.** After taking a breath or two and sitting still for a few, it's time to open the mail. Open the bills, baby. Crunch the numbers. Get all cozy with your bank statements. Look them in the face. Don't let *little fear* keep you in the dark about what's really going on. Been there, done that. It doesn't go away, and it's sending "I'm freaked out and can't handle it" energy to the Universe. Those are not Awesome Life vibes and, truly, there's nothing to fear. You're about to rock this!

- **Get smart.** I'll tell you to read all the books, blogs, and everything you can find on great money habits. Take workshops, go to seminars, and listen to podcasts. But I'll also tell you to look around your close circle. Hello, Rockstar Peeps! Who among your family, friends, and mentors are glowing with money vibes and willing to share their strategies? Ask! This is no time to be embarrassed. You're eating water crackers for dinner, for goodness sake!

- **Create a Money Mission Statement.** What's this about, you ask? It's about deciding and contracting with yourself on how you will receive, manage, grow, and use money to support your purpose and life goals. (See Purpose Statement and Vision Board!) This isn't just for you, it's also a declaration to the Universe that says, "I'm ready! Bring it to me!"

- **Say positive things about money, a.k.a. affirmations!** Yes, I am that person that walks around saying things, like "Money is good!" "I love money!" "I'm receiving money all of the time!" And you know what? It comes. I get random checks out of nowhere, or someone calls and says they want to give me $15,000 just because. True story. Remember, no thoughts or words go unheard. It's all energy you can use to work in your favor. So, come up with your top three affirmations, or just use mine!

- **Make a plan.** A Money Mission Statement is good, but how do you rebuild or build from water crackers without a path? Answer: you don't. It takes thought, structure, patience, vision, time, and a big ol' desire to not stay broke. Let's circle back to the experts you may know, or you may have to look up or stalk to help you. Financial planners are expensive, so I started at the local library. It offered free financial counseling from expert firms in the city. Who knew? You can also check "The Google" and search for the word "FREE." Keep in mind that free doesn't always mean good. This is your money. Do your research and use common sense with whomever you trust, regardless of how little or how much there is right now.

- **Save some.** Yes, you can always save. Yes, you can always save. Even if it's a penny. Yes, you can always save. Put some away for retirement, rainy days, vacations, etc. I have separate savings accounts for a bunch of things, i.e., wedding, family vacations, and entertainment. And most of them started with a penny. Talk with your fancy dancy financial advisor, Rockstar Peep, or that person you've determined can help get you on or back on the path to your Awesome Life.

- **Give some away.** Sharing is caring. I believe we're on Earth to create and to serve others with what we create. Here's where in your Awesome Life journey you build in charitable giving. Here is where you offer up the best of your wallet to someone, someplace, or something. The Universe loves givers, because that's what we are at our core. Give with joy, happiness, and without *little fear*. It's coming back to you a million times over.

You are destined to live a prosperous life—if you want to. If you're willing to get your mind right and excited about the abundance racing toward you, do your work, and let the Universe do its job, you can release this struggle, because it is not meant for you or anyone else for that matter. It's time to get a new wallet!

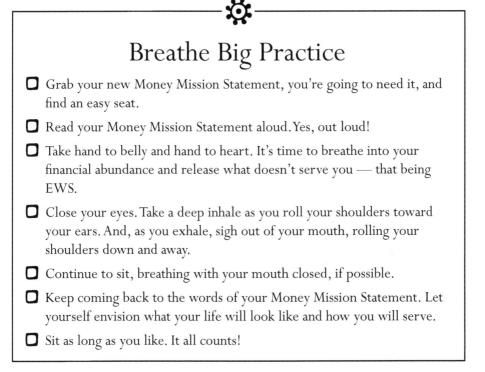

Breathe Big Practice

☐ Grab your new Money Mission Statement, you're going to need it, and find an easy seat.

☐ Read your Money Mission Statement aloud. Yes, out loud!

☐ Take hand to belly and hand to heart. It's time to breathe into your financial abundance and release what doesn't serve you — that being EWS.

☐ Close your eyes. Take a deep inhale as you roll your shoulders toward your ears. And, as you exhale, sigh out of your mouth, rolling your shoulders down and away.

☐ Continue to sit, breathing with your mouth closed, if possible.

☐ Keep coming back to the words of your Money Mission Statement. Let yourself envision what your life will look like and how you will serve.

☐ Sit as long as you like. It all counts!

Live Big Takeaways

- ☐ Empty Wallet Syndrome is not your destiny. Drop it. Let it go.
- ☐ Take inventory of your money drama and decide to make a change, if necessary, to help you achieve your goals and dreams.
- ☐ Develop a Money Mission Statement and a plan to build wealth to serve your purpose and share with others.

Get excited! Pom poms up! High kicks and all that! Throw a party and ceremonially burning of your old wallet, habits, and the rest!

I love money! Say it with me now: "I love money"!

What a relief to release all the negative drama you have with money. It's time to live fully in your destiny and the financial support that's coming your way. You're setting yourself up and those you love for your abundant future.

18

Abundance—Your New Vibe!

"Yes, you do have it all.
Open your eyes."

I used to teach yoga classes at the YMCA in Harlem, New York. There was a lovely, light-of-the-world locker-room attendant who would always come in singing, "Life is beautiful, life is wonderful." Every time I'd see her it was "Life is beautiful, life is wonderful," as she picked up towels, smiled, and chatted with members. "Life is beautiful, life is wonderful." I'd always smile and feel just a bit brighter than I did before she entered. And you know what? Life IS beautiful. Life IS wonderful. She totally got what most of us miss! And this, my love, is that you are already living an abundant Awesome Life. It's inside you and all around you, but perhaps you've just been too caught up in what social media and TV would have you believe is your joy. Ahem! Not real. So not real. Or, at least, not your reality and not your abundance.

If you've been doing the work, sitting, breathing, letting go, letting in, rolling with *little fear* and cousin *doubt*, celebrating the little steps, paying attention, I hope you're starting to get clearer. Starting to wake up. I had to or else I was going to miss it. And you might miss it. The Universe is already rockin' with you and your dreams, goals, purpose, and mission to serve. You're already in your Breathe Big, Live Big world. You're already doing it! Wall Slides, detours, and all. You're manifesting the life you deserve.

What's your abundance song? How are you showing up and owning who you are and where you are on this day? Not yesterday, not tomorrow, but today. And, yes, I'm humming the Broadway-hit *Hamilton* song "The Schuyler Sisters", where they sing about how lucky they are to be alive at that time and place. Abundance is a feeling. It's a state of mind. It's knowing you are provided for and supported in whatever you're doing to rock this life and serve others with your biggest, boldest light.

You're living the life of your dreams right now.

Take a look at your To Thrive list. Whoa! Wait! It's been a minute since we talked about this. Remember, your To Thrive list replaced that dismal, never-ending To Do list. It's just a few or even the one thing you'll do today that helps to support and to move you toward your purpose, Vision, Roadmap, and Awesome Life. Are you doing the things on your To Thrive list? Do they speak to the people that are already with you, loving you, guiding you, supporting you? Are they based on the incredible experiences you are already having and wanting to explore more?

It took more than a few Wall Slides for me to see how absolutely amaze-balls my life is. Right now, at this moment. No, really, it's astoundingly abundant! I'm living in one of the greatest cities on Earth, doing things I love. I'm traveling to places I've never been and saying yes to things I've dreamed that have become real. I'm serving and inspiring people to walk in their truest light and brunching with friends who are rocking this life. I wake up every morning next to my one true heart and help raise a brilliant, beautiful girl into a fabulous woman when I thought I'd slept on that chance. I am abundant! And so are you!

When was the last time you took a pause and looked around at the good, the great, the miraculous things already happening in your life?

The Abundance Gratitude Factor, a.k.a. Add up what's good now and celebrate it!

Don't get so blinded by your fabulous Vision Board and important Roadmap that you're constantly thinking: how can my life get better, because right now it sucks? Been there. Done that. Snore. Do not, and I repeat, do not throw yourself a daily dreaming-of-the-day-my-life-doesn't-totally-blow pity party. Instead, every morning and night survey the landscape of your life.

If abundance is a mindset, then you've got to train your mind to see it. So, it's time to exercise your gratitude muscles each day, twice a day, every moment of every day! Take time to write in your journal, at the top of your To Thrive list, or on a post-it on the bathroom mirror. Note: Remember, writing in red lipstick on mirrors freaks people out.

Spend some time being grateful and thankful for the abundance that exists in your life right now. Even if it's for getting a moment to yourself to read a book or to sit and breathe. I don't know about you, but peace and quiet and a moment to myself are golden! Hello, grateful.

Here are some other things I do to lift me back into a grateful state, when I start seeing myself signing up for the doom-and-gloom tour:

- **Set an "I am grateful! I am abundant!" alarm on your phone.** Each hour or at a specific time of day, set an alarm or calendar event. If you're like me and live by your calendar alerts, then this will be perfect! Personally, I need this when I wake up and go to bed. It's often in a morning or evening haze that I go to my "Ugh, same stuff, new day" mindset or my "Oh when will life get better" mindset. Attach your favorite song, or sound, or photo to it. Get a jolt of "My life is full, wonderful, and amaze-balls!" when you need it.

- **Roses and thorns.** Or better, thorns and then roses. I have to admit, I've only done this once or twice with my family. But I got the idea from Bruce's daughter and I think it's cool. Around the dinner table with your family or friends, have each person share his or her "thorn" (something bad or challenging that day) and "rose" (something good that day). If it's you by your glorious self, write it down or talk it out! I talk to myself all the time, and I'm proud of it!

- **Serve others.** Get out of your head and off your couch. Give your time and energy to help others. Show up and volunteer with a local community charity, house of worship, or school. Offer up smiles, love, and support to someone else. Get perspective.

- **Get still.** Get grateful. Receive abundance. Since you've now practiced at sitting still, it's time to focus your easy-seat time on gratitude. I've got a simple breath exercise at the end of the chapter just for you.

- **Start celebrating what's coming your way!** Can you rejoice in this moment about the abundance you're manifesting? Can you give gratitude to the Universe with a big ol' "Thank You!" for all that's glued, stapled, and taped to your Vision Board that's racing toward you? Try it!

It's time to set the party table for gratitude! The Abundance Gratitude Factor is about announcing to the Universe that wherever you are in life—whether you're at the Wall, getting up from the Wall, or skipping joyfully down your yellow-brick Roadmap toward your goals and dreams— you're thankful for what you have and what's to come. It's about putting your Awesome Life approved stamp on the here and now.

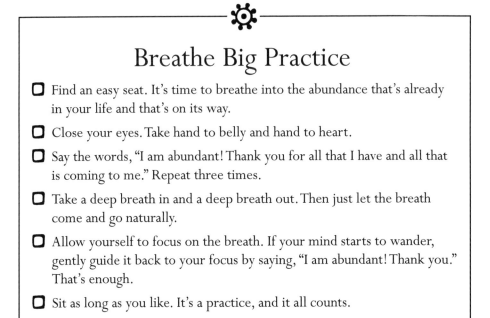

Breathe Big Practice

☐ Find an easy seat. It's time to breathe into the abundance that's already in your life and that's on its way.

☐ Close your eyes. Take hand to belly and hand to heart.

☐ Say the words, "I am abundant! Thank you for all that I have and all that is coming to me." Repeat three times.

☐ Take a deep breath in and a deep breath out. Then just let the breath come and go naturally.

☐ Allow yourself to focus on the breath. If your mind starts to wander, gently guide it back to your focus by saying, "I am abundant! Thank you." That's enough.

☐ Sit as long as you like. It's a practice, and it all counts.

I wake up with "I am abundant! Thank You!" on my lips. You should, too, if you're ready and doing the work to truly take your life and offering to the next level. Get the vibe!

Live Big Takeaways

☐ Let your abundance flag fly! It's time to start vibrating on high and letting the Universe and everyone around you know you are open to receive all you dream.

☐ Use the Abundance Gratitude Factor. Celebrate who and what you already have in your life. Get all sentimental with it. Give hugs and kisses and walk around your studio apartment or big house and take it all in (however little it may be) like you mean it.

☐ If you're not feeling it, use one or all my tips to get in the mood. Invite friends over for a Roses and Thorns party, volunteer to serve food at the homeless shelter, or add an abundance reminder on your phone.

Make sure you're surrounding yourself with Rockstar Peeps who are abundance-minded and support you in your journey. You're going to need that support on days when *little fear*, *doubt* and the rest come knockin'.

Onward, superhero!

.

112 BREATHE BIG LIVE BIG

.

19

When You Look Forward to Mondays with a Yaassss, You're on the Right Path

"Days of the week aren't real. But life is."

A while ago, I decided to take Mondays off.

The good news about being an entrepreneur with a business that's riding high is that you can take any day off, if you want. Wonderful, right? Well, the bad news was that I wasn't riding high. Frankly, I was barely getting by, plus I was in the middle of Costa Rica retreat-registration-and-planning mania. But I had to. I needed to breathe. I needed time to rest, regroup, restart, and get my mind back on my family, Vision Board goals, Roadmap, abundance, fearlessness, and all the rest. I knew that if I didn't take the time, I was headed toward my next Wall Slide. Remember that whole viral meningitis thing? Most importantly, I wanted to start the week with my best "pom poms up," I'm ready to Rock this thing" mindset.

I wanted Mondays to be my "Yaaassssss!" (insert a snap of the fingers here) day. And so, I hesitantly explained to Bruce Almighty I was clearing my schedule of a full day of revenue. Note: At that time, I was the sole revenue source for my business. If I wasn't there, no money would come in, no bills were paid, and no sourcing new business. Snore. That had to change. But I digress.

Regardless of the financial downside, I took my day. At first, I thought, "Why didn't I do this sooner?" I was sleeping in. Well, I was sort of sleeping in, since Bruce Almighty wakes up to go to work at 2:30 AM. But I was waking up at a very decent 7:00 AM, having coffee, doing morning yoga and meditation, baking homemade no-knead bread for my family, having date night, doing all my regrouping and Vision Board loving, going to the dentist, having lunch with friends, and doing "cool-kid" stuff. This regular day-off thing was golden! Or so I thought for about two weeks.

Take a Child's Pose and forget about it. Or, rock a Hand-stand, if that makes you happier.

Fast-forward two weeks and the fun, cool-kid stuff had all but vanished. I was lying around in my pajamas well into the afternoon, checking social media, reading my favorite magazines, texting friends and Bruce Almighty at work, and basically doing my damnedest not to do any of the work I loved. Because, well, it was my special day off and rules are rules. Snore.

I love what I do. No, really, I love showing up each day in person or virtually, sharing my gifts and serving you the way I do. I could do it every day. I could talk about it every day. But, should I work my fingers to the bone and never have a moment's rest or do fun, cool-kid stuff? No, of course not. But, what I realized was that I looked forward to living my life and doing my life's work. It was my "Yaaaasss!" (insert finger snap here) moment. When you wake up each day and want to, crave to, do what you do so fabulously, serving others, with all that you have, you're going the right way. You're on the right the path. You're manifesting that Vision Board and working the hell out of your Roadmap towards your Awesome Life. No. You're living your Awesome Life!

Now, I'm not advocating never taking a day, week, or even a month off. I've done all that when I've really wanted and needed. You need rest. It's underrated, so take it when you need it. That said, I'm talking about having that big bright excitement about your life and what you're doing in your life that makes you want to holler from the rooftops, "Come and get it!"

Bruce Almighty once told me I teach classes and do my motivational talks in my sleep at night sometimes. I laughed and thought, "Perfect!"

Bottle that boomshakalaka feeling!

If there's a goal you want to set, a dream to shoot for, I'd say it's to be able to wake up ready, excited, and willing to do what you dream. It's to be able to look at anyone around you who begrudges Mondays with an "Are you kidding me?" face and a huge smile. Because you've figured out the not-so-secret secret. That is, you've decided to set your goals, planned and prepared, and surrounded yourself with your Rockstar Peeps to ride with joy every day. Mondays included!

I learned a lot about myself and mission with my little Monday experiment. First, I realized I needed new pajamas. Seriously! Second and more importantly, I realized I'd started and restarted myself right into my Awesome Life. Yes, it was challenging. Yes, there were a whole lot of hard lessons learned and a few Wall Slides along the way and probably a few more to come. Yes, I had to let some friends, things, and experiences go along the way. Yes, I constantly carpooled *little fear* and *doubt* around all day every day. But, I loved it! It gave me life.

So how do you bottle that feeling and drink it up each day?

- **Count it all up.** I've said this before. It's about celebrating all the little wins along the way and throwing yourself a party in your head or in real time. Get used to knowing the next win is right at your doorstep and that today's the day!

- **Reboot your Purpose Statement.** If you're not waking up wanting to hit it, check in with what you've committed to do in your life personally and professionally. Maybe things have changed for you. Maybe you're headed in the wrong direction. Every time I look at my statement, it's like a mental energy boost! That's where you want to be.

- **Lock arms with people who love who they are and what they do, a.k.a. Rockstar Peeps!** This Awesome Life stuff is contagious. So, I say this again and again and again, double check who you're hanging out with on a regular basis. (And, yes, that includes family!) Are these people who can't wait to get their day going? Are they excited about their lives, work, whatever's going on? This energy is where it's at and it absolutely fills you, helps to drive you, and keeps you shining.

- **Take time out each day to get still and get real.** Even superheroes have to sit down sometimes and think on things. I cannot say it enough. The answers, the joy, the pep in your step comes from the ability to sit, listen, ask for guidance, take direction, and make better choices that speak to your Vision. This is how you can wake up and say, "Let's go!" It's because you know who you're serving, why you're serving them, where you're going, and how to get there. Take it from a Gemini Type A Yogini, do these Breathe Big exercises and you will discover how your work and life light you up. And, that you might need new pajamas!

Breathe Big Practice

☐ Each morning, after your "Thank You" and moving your body with your yoga practice or whatever works it out, find an easy seat.

☐ Close your eyes and take hand to belly, hand to heart.

☐ Let the breath come and go, feeling your belly rise and fall with each inhale and exhale.

☐ Take this time to set an intention for your day. For example, "Today is the best day of my life! I will show up like I mean it and rock it!" Say it out loud. Note: Get used to speaking what you want and need to the Universe. Say it out loud like you mean it and be heard.

☐ Release your hands and turn your focus back to your breath.

☐ Practice envisioning your day and how it will go. Begin to direct your thoughts to the success of your day. Set the whole scene up! Put yourself in it and imagine it playing out just as you want.

☐ Keep your focus on gently guiding your thoughts back to the positive if they head off in the dark zone of doom and gloom.

☐ Gently release your "fabulous day" thoughts and turn your focus back to your inhale and exhale.

☐ Take as much or as little time as you like with this. It all counts and no one is judging.

Live Big Takeaways

☐ You deserve to wake up with a "Yaaassssss!" on your mind, regardless of the day of the week.

☐ Your life plan (Ahem! That Vision Board and Purpose Statement) should be built to keep that excitement real for you.

☐ When you feel it, bottle it! Take note when you're riding high. Is it because you're following your yellow-brick Roadmap and sharing the love? Is it because you can't imagine doing anything else because this or that feels so good? Hang out with that feeling!

20

Good News—We're in This Thing Together

"Scoot over.
I'm riding with you."

When I was thirteen, my parents bought a brand-new, black-and-silver Dodge Ram van. We were a big family of five kids plus Mom and Dad at the time, so it was perfect for getting us around for activities, church on weekends, and road trips every now and then. It was awesome!

It was also the first car my sisters and I learned to drive. And, boy did we drive that van. My poor parents! We were all over town with one of us at the wheel, while the others hung out the windows looking for friends or, really, just boys. We had a lot of fun and definitely got into a lot of trouble, to put it mildly. We were always together. We always took rides together. Even as moody teenage sisters who couldn't stand each other one minute and really couldn't stand each other the next, we hung out together. All of my most vivid memories of the black-and-silver van are of us rolling with the fun or dealing with the drama. Nevertheless, we were in it together.

I want to be honest with you about my journey and give you as much as I can to prepare and support you on yours. So, I'll tell you this: some days it's going to feel like you're lost in space all by yourself and you're running out of oxygen. You might feel so alone and lost (Hello *little fear*! Ugh!) that you don't know what to do. You might want to eat every ounce of that gallon of ice cream or drink that bottle of wine with a straw to try to fill the void. I'm just sayin'! You might think you're invisible. You're not. This is the van, and we're rolling together. We've got you! We being all of us who are on this Awesome Life journey.

You've got a prize-winning cheer squad rooting for you.

You're only as alone as you allow yourself to be. Make a big ol' note of that and stick it on your mirror! What stories are you telling yourself about how you're doing this all by yourself, or no one helps you, or blah, blah, blah? Been there, done that. Snore.

There's no way you've come this far without family, friends, your Rockstar Peeps, and the coffee-shop barista who makes your perfect Americano. They're all in the van. And when you stop to really think about it and tear into whatever nonsense story you've wrapped around your perceived loneliness on this journey, you'll see it. I've had to. A few times. Usually during or shortly after an Emmy-Award-Winning Wall Slide. I get it. I totally get it.

I ask again: what "I'm-all-by-my-lonesome" stories are you telling yourself? Take a second. Take an hour. Think about it, and then write it down. It's funny how things become real, or in this case, false, when we start to put them down in writing or, even better, speak them out loud. You can use the same exercise we did earlier with money (say it with me: money):

> I'm so alone. — I'm constantly surrounding myself with people who support me and give me amazing energy!

> No one helps me. — I have an abundance of support from {insert names, groups, organizations, etc., Here}.

Get it? Keep going. I bet you'll realize that whatever doubt, *little fear*, and loneliness (who is their fifth cousin on their mother's side) have you believing is a lie. You're covered. You're held. We'll party with you when times are good and be there to catch you when you fall. We'll help you learn from your mistakes so that you won't choose to make them again. We love you and want you to succeed. You just have to see us. You just have to ask us. You just have to come from a place of love and light. That's it. You're not alone. Take the blinders off and put down the ice cream and wine.

In my yoga classes, workshops, and retreats, I have a lot of fun teaching students poses that allow them to take their practice to a new level. My favorites are balancing poses, because with the first few attempts, there's always this complete *little fear* of falling. I can almost hear a collective gasp whenever it's time to balance. So, I always say:

Go for it! You're held. We've got your back.

It's usually when you're stepping into uncharted Awesome Life territory that loneliness comes a-knockin'. Kind of like trying that new Cirque de Soleil yoga balancing pose. It knows you're learning, growing, getting stronger, and opening up to a whole new world and it's not about to let you go there. Hater! That's when you get to tap into the collective "Hell yes! We can do this!" energy.

Let me be as clear as day. Side-eye anyone (including yourself) who tells you they're living and sharing their fullest without the help, love, and support of a cheer squad. They have some sit-still homework to do to get real. It's possible the Universe is about to put some speed bumps in their path to slow them down so they can take a longer look at what's really going on.

Breathe Big Practice

Before you get to your breath practice, I want you to grab that list of accomplishments and victories you wrote down a few chapters ago. Take a few moments to think about all the people who helped you achieve them, such as teachers, friends, and family. Write down their names. Visualize their faces. See them riding along with you on your journey. Begin to picture your new squad members you'll pick up along the way. Think about the goals you've envisioned and the people you'll need to help you get there.

☐ Find that easy seat again and close your eyes.

☐ Take hand to belly, hand to heart. Breathe.

☐ Visualize your existing cheer squad and those who are coming your way. Repeat the phrase, aloud: "I am held. I am supported. I am loved." Say it three times and then release it.

☐ Continue to focus on your breath as you sit quietly for as long as you'd like. It all counts.

Live Big Takeaways

☐ You're never alone. You have all the support you need. Just take a deep breath and look around.

☐ Change your mind about loneliness. It's just the ego, *little fear* and the cronies trying to hold you back from your biggest joys. Each time you have a thought that goes there, reframe it. There are a whole bunch of folks in the van with you!

☐ Rock hard with the faith that your cheer squad has your back.

☐ Show up and take the next step knowing the Awesome Life community is taking it with you.

21

Never, No, NEVER, Give Up!

"You can whine.
You can cry.
But you can't quit."

My niece Olivia ran for class representative in 3rd and 4th grade and lost. In 5th grade she upped her game and ran for vice president of the whole school and won! I love this for so many reasons. First, she's my BFF Betsy's first-born, to whom we refer as my surrogate child because we're so much alike. Second, that's the stuff Rockstars are made of. So proud of her!

When I moved to New York, one of my dreams was to be a featured teacher at one of the biggest yoga events in the world, Solstice in Times Square, Mind Over Madness Yoga, where thousands do yoga in the middle of the craziness. At the time, I wasn't formally trained to teach so I just attended, grabbed my mat space in a side ditch, and imagined myself up on the stage. After becoming certified, I got a random email from a yoga teacher friend of mine, Pepper, which simply said, "You should do this" with a Craigslist link to an announcement. It was an audition announcement for webcast hosts for the Solstice. "Hmmm, well, that's great, but I really want to teach," I unenthusiastically shared with Bruce Almighty that day. He said, "Do it! You'll be perfect." So, on my birthday, I walked into the audition and got the gig.

For three years, I served as webcast host and event announcer for the Solstice. And for three years, I asked to be considered to teach the masses. Didn't happen. No problem. It was on my Vision Board, I had a plan I was working, and I was breathing and sitting still with it. It was coming. Plus, I was enjoying my time, working with amazing people, and doing something I'd never done before. To top it off, I was also great at it!

The next year rolled around, and again I pitched teaching. And again, the answer was a very kind: "We've filled all our teaching spots." No problem. It was coming.

Out of the blue, in the middle of a sunny spring afternoon, I got a call back. "We have a spot for you. Would you like to kick off this year's Solstice by teaching the first class of the day?" Ha! "Absolutely!" I responded. Pom poms up and smooches to the Universe!

Don't panic. It's all coming to you.

I'm not a quitter. No, I'm really not good at quitting at all. Apparently, my niece Olivia is my spirit animal! No, no quit in me. Not with the stuff that speaks to my soul and helps me to help others. As a matter of fact, my hard-headedness and my "Oh, yes, this is going to happen!" stubbornness has sometimes gotten me into trouble, debt, drama, relationship breaks, and thrown me right into a good Wall Slide or two. But I've kept going. Truth is I've had plenty of little fear and doubt attacks with that quitter voice screaming, "Run for the hills!" But, thankfully, my yoga practice, my meditation practice, my super-amazing guy, my Rockstar Peeps, my best friends, and all of you have supported me and kept me on this journey.

Remember, we're all in this thing together! It helps to know that you know and walk in and live your purpose each day. Practice keeping your eyes set on your vision. It may feel so much easier to quit, walk away, and go back to your less than Awesome Life, but it's not. Quitting rains down all kinds of hot mess-ness on your brain, on your heart, and on your soul. It drains you of your superhero power a little or a lot each time. You are bigger than any obstacle. Keep going.

Give it one more breath.

I often ask my yoga students to stay in a pose for just one more breath. "Hold on and see where the next breath might lead," I say. In the past when I used to coach recovering drug addicts to run marathons, I would say basically the same thing: "Just run to the next mile marker. We'll see what happens from there." Even if you stutter, stumble, or fall flat on your face on this journey, get up. Even when you feel like you've lost everything, move forward. Even when everyone tells you no, ask again. What I've learned and continue to learn is that it may not come in the timing you thought or in the packaging you expected, but it will come and it will be just right, if you stay the course. Breathe, then start or restart. Time to tap into your power. Your light might get dimmed for a moment, but this too shall pass, Rockstar. You have what it takes, and you are preparing yourself for the detours and perceived roadblocks everyday with your Vision and Roadmap. You don't get to quit. It's too important and your life is valuable. You are here to share your love, talents, and gifts. You can't sit on the sidelines in a puddle of "It was too hard!" or "It isn't what I planned," or "They laughed at me." Breathe, then start or restart.

So, the next time you feel ready to abandon your Awesome Life journey:

- **Make quitting a non-option.** This really has to happen at the start or the restart. You have to believe and want the change in direction of your life so much that giving up is just not part of the equation. Gwenna called me to the carpet with a question when I was going through a hard time in my business and personal life. She asked, "So, are you planning an exit or planning a win?" Plan to win. Period. Non-negotiable.

- **Remember, it's no fun to take a ride in the Sweeper Bus.** If you've ever run in marathons or distance races, you know this bus picks up injured runners, those who take longer than the prescribed time allowed on the course, and those who just quit. I've been on that bus with a runner I coached during the New York Marathon. He broke his foot during the race, so there was definite cause. That said, the Sweeper Bus is no-joke sad. OMG! You could hear a pin drop on that bus. Just sad. Most of all, you could feel the drained energy and see the looks on the faces of those who decided it was too much, too hard, and they couldn't make it. Disheartening. You don't belong there. You can do it!

- **Breathe. It's just one moment in time. You'll get through.** Sometimes we get caught up in the belief that we're in a never-ending, Groundhog-Day loop of pain, suffering, and personal and professional disasters. Snore. As I've said before, keep breathing, stuff changes.

- **Pour yourself a beverage and reminisce about the good times.** Indulge in a glass of wine, cup of tea or coffee, green juice, or water. Take a walk down memory lane of all the times you wanted to, but didn't, give up, and you and those you love and serve were better off. Option to add a "Boom!" out loud after each one. You're welcome!

- **Again, with the affirmations?** Yep! It's time to turn up the volume on those positive words and sayings. Don't hold back. Put them on repeat and post them everywhere. This is emergency surgery!

- **Lean into it, but just for a bit.** Examine what it feels like to want to stop, drop, and quit. It's pretty ugly. I know. Been there, done that. But get cozy with it for just a bit. Try to come at it as though you're having an out-of body-experience. See it from the outside looking in. There's something to learn. The Universe is probably offering some "what to do" and some "what not to do again" tips. Get perspective.

- **Know the difference between "Letting Go" and "Quitting."** Oh, this is a good one! The ego loves to try to pass off quitting as "releasing" or "letting go" of something that's not serving. There is a difference. When you release something because it's toxic and blocking your joy and light, it may be difficult or hard, but there's a lift, a little rainbow high that comes from dropping it. When you quit, it sits with you forever and gnaws at you forever. Yeah, they're different, right?

Breathe Big Practice

☐ When you start to head to, as I like to call it, the Quitter Zone, it's because you've gotten away from the core of who you are. You've forgotten your Rockstar power. So, again, come back to your easy seat. Get still. The answers are in that space.

☐ Take a hand to belly, a hand to heart.

☐ First, just notice the strength and consistency of your heartbeat. Whew! Still alive. That's the good news, because everything can and will change with the next beat of your heart. Just hang out here. Eyes closed, sitting tall, and just allowing.

☐ Let your belly rise and fall and ride that wave as well.

☐ Let your mind focus on your goals and dreams and the people who you will serve. Release any negative thoughts that come to mind and gently get back to the good stuff.

☐ Stay as long as you like. Remember, it all counts! Just stay in your practice.

Live Big Takeaways

☐ No quitting allowed! That is all.

I know you've heard it a lot—never give up and don't quit—and there's a reason. Your cheer squad, your Rockstar Peeps, and all of us on this journey totally get how if you make it an option, you'll go there and miss or leave behind everything and everyone that will completely light up your life. Stay the course. It's so worth it!

22

Receive.
Say Thank You.
Love.

"What if you really can get what you ask for?"

Along with my Vision Board, I have a Creation Box where I literally drop my wishes, dreams, and goals in whenever I'm feeling it. I got the idea from *Ask and It Is Given*, by Esther and Jerry Hicks. I loved it and went with it. I write them on small pieces of paper and drop in photos and images from magazines, blogs, etc. that I read. Then I place them in the Creation Box and allow the Universe to go to work, while I light my life up and share that light every day to the best of my ability. Early this year, I decided I really wanted to make Bruce Almighty and I "official." I wrote on the back of an old bytracye business card, "Bruce will propose to me this summer in Paris," dropped it in, and went on loving him and our family with all that I had. I would allow the Universe to do what it does. And it did! And I'm not surprised.

It was a proposal of a lifetime on an apartment rooftop in Le Marais overlooking a glittering Eiffel Tower. Wow! It was out of this world. And, I asked for it!

If you've been reading this book and doing the work, it's because you're ready for something different, something more, something bigger and better than the life you're living today. You're creating the life you dream and deserve. And you can have it.

Ask for what you want and for what you know in your heart is true. Show up. Love. Then allow and watch your magic happen.

I wrote this book because I really am fired up about living my most abundant life and inspiring others to do the same. And, as we come to this last chapter, I need you to know that it's available to everyone. It's completely yours for the living. But not everyone believes it, works it, and, this is the good part, receives it when it's right in front of them. That's the difference between those of us who are steering our course each day with purpose and vision and those who have decided to walk around blindfolded, trying to hit the piñata of this Awesome Life. Doesn't work that way. I've tried it. More than once. Snore.

I've given you a few tools to get you going and keep you focused as you jump on to this new, exciting path. And it is exciting! It's all of that and more. And the main ingredient is you. You are the success factor. Remember, you're the magic. Your ability to stay open and available to what comes with the next breath is the key. Your willingness to say "Yes!" to your dreams and goals when you really want to run and hide in the closet is vital. Your strength to get back up after hitting the Wall is critical. Your fearlessness to walk with your heart and soul wide open so that you can take in all the love and abundance that's racing toward you and give it back is everything. You are doing this thing, love!

It's time to recap and make sure you're off to a good start or restart on your Awesome Life journey:

- **Dream big and take action.** Each day, take one step to move yourself further along your path and toward your goals. Even the smallest steps count and can lead to big leaps in time. When in *doubt* or in *little fear*, do something. Anything.

- **Define your purpose.** Tell yourself and the Universe where you want to go, who you want to go with, and who you want to serve. No purpose? No direction.

- **Design your Vision Board.** Paint the boldest, brightest picture of your Awesome Life and put it on walls, screensavers, and wherever you look. See it as real. Name it and claim it!

- **Create your Roadmap.** This is key. You have to know where you're going. Plot out the journey and wrap your focus around the details of getting there. You don't need to know all the "how you're going to get there" stuff, just get the plan down on paper.

- **Prepare your body for the journey.** Get moving! Work, respect, and love your temple of a body. You need all your strength and flexibility to share your talents and gifts and to deal with detours and roadblocks.

- **Count on your Rockstar Peeps.** Pom poms up for the people you already know and will meet along the way who will encourage, console, teach, and love you. You need them and they need you.

- **Sit. Get Still. Breathe. Ask for guidance.** It's a practice that has changed my life and it will yours if you do just that—practice.

- **Drop what's holding you back.** Release those things, people, and situations that are toxic and you know do not serve your journey. It's time. Really, let them go and make room for light.

- **Get your head right about the value of money.** Dive into your beliefs about money and start to wrap your head around how it impacts the quality of your journey and ability to serve and share with others. Yes! Time to give money some love.

- **Know your power.** Remember that you were born fearless and made to soar in this life. You're a superhero. It's in all of us. Give your wings a shine and get busy flying. The clock is ticking on this life. Don't waste it on mediocre.

- **Release the struggle.** Know that what you believe is what will be. What you think, you will do. Decide to let go of limiting beliefs and negative thoughts. You don't have to carry them. Let go. You've got this.

- **Let *doubt* and *little fear* ride along.** Don't waste your time trying to block out the voices. Let them come, as long as they keep quiet and keep their hater energy to themselves. Continue to take action, breathe like a champ, and watch your light shine brighter.

- **I deserve it!** Get used to saying it. All day, every day. This is about you starting or restarting to believe that the world, the Universe, is on your side and wants abundance for you. Say it with me now: "I deserve it!"

- **Be grateful.** You are already tremendously blessed. Really, you are! Take inventory of all that you have in your life today. Be sure to share the I love yous and thank yous freely. Gratitude is the key!

- **Quitting is not an option.** Never give up. Fall down, get back up. Take a break, but come back after your 15 minutes. Never give up. There's too much at stake. This is your life and you're building your dream. You can do it!

- **Open your arms wide and take it all in.** Get in the beautiful habit of receiving what you've asked for. No thought goes unheard and no action goes unseen by the Universe. If you're putting it out there, it's going to come back to you. So, get ready. Get set. Here comes your Awesome Life.

I'm not leaving you high and dry, love! Remember, I'm on the journey too! We're creating this Awesome Life together. I'll be sharing all kinds of helpful tips and motivational "Keep going!" and "Get up! Time to make the Awesome Life!" self-help good stuff at bytracye.com. Stay tuned. In the meantime, I need you to do me a big favor. This is going to do everything to boost your energy for your journey. No, really! You've come this far.

Now, it may sound a little, or maybe a lot yoga funky hippy-like, so stick with me on this. Okay, here it is…

Tell 10 people you LOVE them today.

Boomshakalaka boom! That's it! Love. Tell 10 people you love them today. Call, text, write, Skype, Facetime, or whatever it takes. Show 10 people some love today.

Why 10? I don't know, I just came up with that number out of the blue one day. But this, really, is about getting back to the idea of what matters most, what is our true superhero power, and what truly drives this Awesome Life van. It's love. It has always been and it will always be.

Honestly, it has taken me years to get to this place where I know that my "love practice" has to be front and center. It's all that counts. It may seem hard at times to keep your arms around it. Know that I know this. I'm on the journey, too. But, you've got to sit with it. Breathe with it. Walk with it. Know that when you start and restart with love, you'll go much further and give more sincerely from your most authentic place. And that's what it's all about, baby!

As you're getting your strategies, tips, and tricks together to rock this life and share all your goodness with the world, keep love at the center of it. Give it freely and receive it abundantly, okay?

I love you.

Made in the USA
Middletown, DE
02 May 2021

38848727R00080